Relapse Prevention for Addictive Behaviours

A Manual for Therapists

Also of interest

TREATING DRINKERS AND DRUG USERS IN
THE COMMUNITY
T. A. N. Waller
0-632-03575-7

COGNITIVE THERAPY FOR
DEPRESSION AND ANXIETY
I. M. Blackburn & K. M. Davidson
0-632-03986-8

CHANGING EATING AND
EXERCISE BEHAVIOUR
P. Hunt & M. Hillsdon
0-632-03927-2

SUBSTANCE USE AND MISUSE
G. H. Rassool
0-632-04884-0

Relapse Prevention for Addictive Behaviours

A Manual for Therapists

Shamil Wanigaratne
BSc, DipPsych, CPsychol

Wendy Wallace
BS, MSc, CPsychol, AFBPS

Jane Pullin
SRN, RMN

Francis Keaney
MB, MICGP

Roger Farmer
MD, MSc, MRCP, MRCPsych

FOREWORD BY
Professor G.A. Marlatt

Blackwell
Science

© Shamil Wanigaratne, Wendy Wallace, Jane
Pullin, Francis Keaney and Roger Farmer 1990

Editorial offices:
Blackwell Science Ltd, 9600 Garsington Road, Oxford OX4 2DQ, UK
 Tel: +44 (0)1865 776868
Blackwell Publishing Inc., 350 Main Street, Malden, MA 02148-5020, USA
 Tel: +1 781 388 8250
Blackwell Science Asia Pty, 550 Swanston Street, Carlton, Victoria 3053, Australia
 Tel: +61 (0)3 8359 1011

First published 1990
Reprinted 1995, 1997, 1999, 2002, 2003

ISBN 0-632-02484-4

British Library Cataloging-in-Publication Data
Relapse prevention for addictive behaviours.
   1. Addiction Therapy.
   1. Wanigaratne, Shamil
   616.8606

Set by SNP Best-set Typesetter Ltd., Hong Kong
Printed and bound in India using acid-free paper
by Thomson Press (I) Ltd, India

For further information on Blackwell Publishing, visit our website:
www.blackwellpublishing.com

Contents

Foreword

by

Professor G. A. Marlatt

Professor and Director
Addictive Behaviours Research Unit
University of Washington, Seattle

People often ask me how to define relapse prevention (RP). What is it, exactly? Is it treatment? Prevention? How much does it differ from other approaches such as Alcoholics Anonymous? Readers of this present manual are provided with an excellent introductory overview of the theoretical foundations of the RP model in the first chapter, and I will not go over the same ground here. Rather, I'd like to respond to these questions via a broader perspective in these brief remarks. Let's examine each of these three questions in turn.

(1) Is RP a *treatment* for addiction? RP derives from several sources. One important source is behaviour therapy. As a psychologist trained in behaviourism, I was steeped in the 'dustbowl empiricism', a tradition that favoured research over armchair speculation. In later years as the 'cognitive revolution' and the influence of social learning theory grew, a hybrid cognitive–behavioural approach to behaviour change emerged. So, yes, RP is a 'treatment' in the sense of the term 'therapy'. But RP does not fit the usual medical model of treatment for addictions, in which a 'doctor' or other treatment-provider provides medication or some other medical regimen to the 'patient' (addict). A better analogy for RP is the teacher/student relationship, in which the therapist plays the role of teacher, guide or coach.

Addiction is a trap that only the imprisoned slave (to one's habits) can escape. The RP therapist's job is to teach clients how to free themselves from entrapment in the habit web. With its basis in learning theory, RP fits with a psychoeducational approach to habit change.

(2) Is RP *prevention*? The 'P' in 'RP' would so indicate. At first glance, RP has a prevention goal: to prevent relapse. On the other hand, the practice of RP is focused on the client's ongoing *process* of change, as opposed to a fixed treatment *goal* such as permanent abstinence. I often describe RP as a *maintenance strategy*, a method to work with the ongoing process (including lapses, relapses, and prolapses) that people

experience as they change their behaviour. Like other cognitive–behavioural models, RP can be applied for a variety of behaviour change goals. In our 1985 book, *Relapse Prevention*, Judith Gordon and I defined RP as a *tertiary prevention* programme. Once the addiction problem has become firmly established and the client has selected an abstinence goal (e.g., to stop smoking), RP methods can be employed to enhance the maintenance of initial abstinence, to keep the problem from 'getting worse' as in a tertiary prevention approach. But RP programmes have also been applied in *secondary prevention* programmes in which the goal is to minimise the harm of potentially addictive behaviours (e.g., to moderate food or alcohol intake). Our current research programme in secondary prevention at the University of Washington is geared towards the development of skills-training and lifestyle change for young adults at risk because of current heavy drinking or family history of alcohol dependence. To the extent that coping skill training can be applied to prevent initial drug use or early development of dependence, RP methods can also be used for *primary prevention* goals. Since the emphasis on prevention stems from a public health perspective on addictive behaviours (as distinct from the emphasis on treatment in the disease model), RP is congruent with a focus on health psychology of teaching self-management skills to prevent disease.

(3) Is RP similar to AA or other self-help groups? Some AA members have told me that what goes on in AA is similar to what RP advocates – common interest in the 'here and now' process ('One Day A Time' says AA), a shared focus on learning warning signals (AA says: 'HALT' – don't get too hungry, angry, lonely, or tired), on cognitive coping (an AA slogan to prevent relapse is 'thinking through the drink'), and a common interest in group process and support. Despite these similarities, important differences arise between the two approaches. AA adopts a progressive disease model in which the victim cannot recover except through lifelong fellowship in the group and a continued reliance on a 'higher power' as a means of combatting the 'lower power' of addiction. In the USA, promoters of the disease model have helped spawn many victims who firmly believe that alcoholism or other addictions are caused by genetic and biological abnormalities beyond the control of the addict. From the RP perspective, addictive habits can be changed and the person can 'move on' to other challenges, leaving the addiction behind. In the progressive disease model, the afflicted individual is always on the verge of succumbing to the inevitable downward pull of the disease – always 'recovering', never 'recovered'. An alternative RP slogan: 'I'm discovering, not recovering'.

RP and AA do share a common interest in *self-help*. In AA, members gain valuable support from others sharing in the process of recovery. Just being in the presence of others with the same problem who are helping each other get over it is a source of both inspiration and strong social support. RP is often conducted in group settings as well, although it can also be done in the traditional therapist/client dyad. Coping skills and cognitive restructuring are perhaps more easily learned in a group setting, where social learning and vicarious experiences act to reinforce new habit patterns. Learning new skills in an active setting of group support is an *empowerment* process. Unlike AA with its emphasis on past wrongdoings (e.g., the 'drunkalogue confession'), RP is focused on the future: learning new ways of adapting, with an emphasis on prevention and planning ahead. The philosophy of an RP group is guided by the assumption that addiction is a *challenge* to growth, not a disease that pulls one backward and downward. If life is a series of challenges to be overcome, the challenge of addiction is unique. Addictive behaviours can kill – bad habits can become killer behaviours; that's the challenge. But unlike other 'diseases' addictive behaviour can be overcome by the person's own individual efforts. People *do* change sexual or aggressive behaviour, they *do* change habits. Many addictive behaviours are transformed on the person's own initiative, without receiving formal treatment or participating in a 12-step group. In part, the RP model is patterned after the *natural history* of habit change. As such, RP attempts to accelerate and facilitate this natural process of change. It does so by teaching principles and methods of *self-management* or *self-control* learned from people who have gone through the change process. RP is a method of learning from our mistakes as well as our successes.

Shamil Wanigaratne and his co-authors of this present manual have done an excellent job in laying out the basic structure and practical application of RP. Like any good manual, this one provides both an overview of the problem (addiction), followed by a hands-on 'how to' description of RP methods in action, from recognising high-risk situations for relapse to balancing the client's daily lifestyle. As with the maintenance manual of an automobile, the reader/driver is provided with a 'troubleshooting' section to outline what to do when things go wrong (as they always do). Careful reading of this manual will help therapists educate their clients in the art of autoregulation, or how to be better drivers on the highway to freedom.

Preface

This manual was written to provide a practical guide on how to work with relapse for the 'coal face' workers in the field of addictions. Relapse is an anathema for those who work in the field, for it is generally considered to be the most common outcome of treatment. It is only during the past decade that research has become focused on the problem of relapse. This has resulted in many exciting new developments.

Relapse prevention is one such recent development. The term was coined by Professor G. Alan Marlatt who described it as a collection of cognitive–behavioural strategies and lifestyle change procedures aimed at preventing relapse in addictive behaviours. The use of these strategies is determined by a model of relapse derived from research findings. Much of the literature on relapse prevention at present is theoretical in nature and there is a pressing need for practical guides for its clinical application. We hope this manual will make a contribution towards filling that gap.

The project started with the translation of theoretical material on the subject into session plans to run groups in a community alcohol service. The clients in those first groups and subsequent groups are largely responsible for the development of this manual. Not only did they respond with enthusiasm to this particular approach, they also gave us invaluable feedback and information about its potential use.

The idea of a manual arose from attempts to collate the session plans and the information and feedback provided by the clients into a 'package' to help other members of the team at the Alcohol Problem Advisory Service, University College Hospital, London, which included, nurses, a doctor, a psychiatrist, a psychologist and students from various disciplines, run groups. Being a multidisciplinary team the members had different backgrounds and different depths of knowledge and experience. We wanted to produce a manual that could be easily used by anyone. This idea snowballed into quite a lengthy undertaking. The process was drawn out by a number of factors that included, some members of the team taking up new posts, continuous revamping of the material as a result of experience gained by using relapse prevention with different addictions and in different settings, and countless practical difficulties. We hope this manual will be of use to anyone working in the field of addiction ranging from voluntary workers, care assistants, members of the clergy to professionals such as nurses, social workers, doctors, psychologists and psychiatrists.

Numerous people have helped and contributed towards this project and we cannot thank them all individually. We are particularly indebted to Christine Burke whose limitless energy and patience helped get the manuscript into shape. We would also like to thank Sybil Hunot and the late Peter Hunot and all our work colleagues for their help. Susan Salas, Stewart Wallace, Robert Wallace, Richard Whittaker and Elaine Arnold had the unenviable task of supporting us during this protracted period enduring considerable disruption in their lives. This is much appreciated. We would also like to thank Professor Marlatt for his encouragement. Last but not least we would like to thank all our clients from whom we have learnt so much.

S.W., W.W., J.P., F.K., & R.F.

How To Use This Manual

This manual is intended to be a practical guide to conducting relapse prevention programmes for any type of addictive behaviour. It is based on the cognitive/behavioural model of relapse proposed by Marlatt and Gordon (1985). For those who are not familiar with the model, a brief introduction to background and theory relating to this approach is provided. Those requiring more in depth theoretical background are referred to appropriate sources.

It is the intention of the authors that this manual should facilitate the use of relapse prevention in a wide range of settings, by a wide range of professional groups and care workers. We have attempted to keep jargon to a minimum. A glossary is provided for some of the terms we have used. The 'Trouble Shooting' chapter describes some 'pitfalls' and problems we encountered in running relapse prevention groups.

The manual describes how to plan and conduct groups. Each chapter contains an introduction/notes for therapists, a session timetable and a handout that could be given to clients. Although the manual is written for a group mode, the model and the sessions can easily be translated for individual client work.

The material in the manual is only intended to be a guide to conducting programmes. We hope that therapists will use this guide creatively!

Chapter 1

Introductory Overview

This chapter describes the basic concepts of relapse prevention, recent trends in the study of addictive behaviours, and the cognitive behavioural model of relapse and its applications. It also deals with issues of evaluation and assessment.

What is relapse prevention?

The term is used in this manual to refer to a wide range of strategies to prevent relapse in the field of addictive behaviours. This includes cognitive (thinking) and behavioural techniques used with gamblers, overeaters, etc., as well as what is thought of as the traditional addictive behaviours, e.g. problem drinking, drug abuse. This approach is primarily based on a theoretical model of the relapse process proposed by Marlatt and Gordon (1985).

The emphasis is squarely on self management and the techniques and strategies are aimed at enhancing maintenance of 'habit change'. Relapse prevention can be summed up as a self-control programme that combines behavioural skills training, cognitive interventions and lifestyle change procedures.

Relapse prevention can be used to help clients with any addictive behaviour. We have used this approach with:

Problem drinkers	Criminal re-offenders
Gamblers	Drug users
Addictive sexual behaviours	Smokers
Overeaters	Compulsive spenders

This is by no means an exhaustive list. We know of others who have used these ideas and techniques with a range of problem behaviours/ groups for example: sexual offenders, aggressive outbursts and tranquilliser users. The reader will no doubt find many other applications for this approach.

What relapse prevention means to the client

For the client relapse prevention would mean a specific maintenance programme and a global lifestyle change programme. The goals of a specific maintenance programme can be listed as follows:

- To equip the client with 'skills' to identify, anticipate, avoid/and or cope with high-risk situations.
- If and when a slip (violation) were to occur, to equip the person with the skills and strategies to avoid it becoming a full-blown relapse.
- To increase the client's sense of self-efficacy.

The goals for global lifestyle change can be listed as follows:

- To identify sources of stress in lifestyle.
- To identify and change unhealthy habit patterns.
- To discover and take up positive activities.
- To learn more effective time management (to fill up the vacuum left by giving up addictive behaviour).
- To arrive at a 'moderate' or 'balanced' lifestyle.

The role of the therapist

A therapist working within the relapse prevention framework would aim to help the client achieve these goals by:

- Increasing the client's self-awareness.
- Teaching cognitive/behavioural skills and coping strategies.

In our experience, we have found it most helpful for the therapist to view him or her self as primarily a communicator – a teacher, a seminar leader, a tutor or a guide who is helping the client to help themselves. Relapse prevention provides a different perspective for looking at problems, the therapist communicating a positive message with an optimistic outlook.

To be able to do this effectively:

(1) The therapist must have a clear understanding of the model so that the rationale can be clearly communicated to the client.
(2) The therapist must be familiar with various cognitive and behavioural strategies used.
(3) The therapist must have good communication skills.

This manual aims to provide therapists, of varying degrees of experience and expertise, with the basic tools to carry out relapse prevention work. It is not intended to be restrictive or to be used in a concrete manner. Marlatt and Gordon's model offers much scope for innovation. It is hoped that the manual will inspire therapists to be creative and develop new interventions. We envisage that even the less experienced therapists will combine the material in the manual with their own ideas and skills. Relapse prevention work should be an exciting and rewarding learning experience for both the client and the therapist.

What type of prevention?

The traditional public health model of prevention identifies three levels of prevention:

- *Primary prevention*, which refers to the removal of the cause of a disorder to prevent its occurrence.
- *Secondary prevention*, which refers to the early identification and treatment of a disorder to arrest its progress.
- *Tertiary prevention*, which refers to the treatment of a developed disorder to arrest its development or reduce risk of relapse.

The utility of such a model for addictive disorders where the causes and environmental interrelationships are not always clear has been questioned (Blane, 1976; Kalb, 1975). Taking problem drinking as an example, primary prevention in a simplistic sense would mean prohibition or banning the sale of alcohol. Nevertheless in a broad sense, health education programmes, especially such programmes aimed at school children, can be considered as primary prevention (Alden, 1980). Similarly, health education and treatment programmes aimed at young adults, drink drivers, etc., fit the definition of secondary prevention (Bear *et al.*, 1988). In its original application relapse prevention clearly fits the definition of tertiary prevention, i.e. reducing relapse risk of an established addictive behaviour. Nevertheless it has been argued that the approach can equally be applied to both primary and secondary preventative work as well (Marlatt and Gordon, 1989). The application of relapse prevention techniques and strategies in AIDS risk reduction (Roffman *et al.*, 1988) is an example of this.

Addictive behaviours

Any human activity has the potential of becoming an *addictive behaviour*. Some of these activities can be described as *negative addictions* because they are judged to be harmful to the individual or to society. Harm to the individual is judged in physical, mental and social terms. Substance misuse, gambling, overeating and forms of sexual behaviours are often classed as negative addictions.

The term *addiction* often implies a *loss of control* on the part of the individual and a certain *compulsion* to engage in the activity. This carried out to extremes is judged harmful to the individual and those around him. There is also an implication of *distress* to the individual if prevented from engaging in the activity.

The unified concept of *addictive behaviours* describing such seemingly diverse activities as drinking, smoking, heroin use, gambling, eating and sexual practices is a relatively recent development (Orford, 1985; Brownell *et al.*, 1986). Previously each of these activities was studied in isolation and described in unique and concrete terms.

Recent developments in the field

The last few years have seen something of a revolution in the field of addictions. The breaking down of barriers and the resulting cross-fertilisation of ideas between the disciplines has heralded an exciting new era. This comes at a time when the world is waking up to the cost of negative addictions, in both human and economic terms, e.g. problem drinking, compulsive sexual behaviours and IV drug use in the spread of HIV infection.

The emergent field of *holistic or behavioural medicine* has had a major influence on recent developments. The integration of medical, psychological and sociological worlds combining in treatment approaches that were hitherto used in isolation does not simplify the work of the therapist or clinician. There are major implications for both assessment and treatment of addictive behaviours. These will be explored in more detail later.

The limitations of the medical viewpoint alone can be demonstrated by taking a particular approach to problem drinking. Clinicians adhering to a biological or disease model tended to concentrate in their assessment of causation largely on genetic or familial factors. Treatment placed undue emphasis on 'detoxification', using drugs to offset withdrawal effects. The predominant underlying assumption (Jellineck, 1960) had been that once such a detoxified individual consumed alcohol, after a period of abstinence, the physical make-up of the individual was such that he or she would soon revert to pretreatment levels of drinking. The assessment and treatment process largely ignored the psychological and social world of the individual. There is strong evidence pointing to a genetic link in problem drinking (Goodwin, 1985) and differences in the physiological make-up of problem drinkers in the way they metabolise alcohol (Schuckit, 1987).

On the other hand there are a number of studies showing that even previously severely dependent problem drinkers can continue to drink at drastically reduced levels following treatment (Heather and Robertson, 1981; Sobel and Sobel, 1978). This illustrates the point that while the biological model may hold some truth, it is not the whole truth. By the same token some psychological approaches also concentrate on a very narrow field. Certain behavioural approaches, e.g. aversion therapy, concentrate almost totally on stimulus response factors almost to the exclusion of other psychological factors such as mood, conflicts, identity and social environment.

The research findings on controlled drinking (Heather and Robertson, 1981) have had far reaching consequences which go beyond the area of problem drinking. This has had the effect of shattering the established view on the subject that had prevailed for decades. The established view had total abstinence as the only goal of treatment and all outcomes of interventions were measured by this very strict yardstick. The controlled drinking findings have generated a much more flexible approach to treatment. This has enabled therapists to work out genuine individual goals with clients.

Communality across addictive behaviours

Outside the area of problem drinking the findings on controlled drinking have contributed to a communality movement in the study of addictions. Previously the term addiction was almost exclusively used to describe excessive drinking or drug abuse. The applicability of a total abstinence treatment goal to these behaviours is one possible explanation for this. Of course total abstinence is not a viable treatment goal for overeating. Similarly total abstinence applied to sexual behaviours could have drastic effects on the population. The demonstration of the possibility of 'control' or 'limiting excesses' in the area of problem drinking invited researchers to look at common factors and possible common treatments across addictions (Orford, 1985; Brownell *et al.*, 1986). This has had many positive outcomes. It has enabled therapists to transfer and adapt skills gained in one area of addiction to another. It has enabled therapists to deal with issues such as 'multiple addictions', 'addiction substitution' and 'addictive cycles' in a comprehensive way for the first time. New perspectives such as viewing 'lifestyle imbalance' as an antecedent or a major factor in maintaining addictive behaviours have emerged (Marlatt and Gordon, 1985).

The view of communality across addictive behaviours is a central element in the relapse prevention approach described in this manual. Its relevance is twofold:

(1) The same formula for maintenance of change could be used for any addictive behaviour.
(2) Lifestyle change, which is a key element in relapse prevention, is a fundamental change irrespective of the addiction in focus.

The 'holistic' nature of the relapse prevention approach offers the therapist a comprehensive way of dealing with problems such as addictive cycles and addiction substitution.

What is an addiction?

A return to this fundamental question is necessitated by the recent developments in the field described above. An individual who has an addiction could simply be described as someone with an 'excessive appetite' for that activity (Orford, 1985). From such a general perspective an acceptable definition needs to be equally applicable to behaviours ranging from overeating and gambling to alcohol and substance abuse. This is quite understandably a tall order.

Using research findings and published work in the field (e.g. Peel, 1985; Shaffer and Milkman, 1985), Donovan and Marlatt (1988) have derived a definition to cater to this requirement. They define an 'addiction' as a complex, progressive behaviour pattern having biological, psychological, sociological and behavioural components. They see such a pattern differing from others by the individual's overwhelmingly pathological involvement in or attachment to it, subjective compulsion to continue it, and reduced ability to exert control over it. An addictive behaviour pattern continues despite its negative impact on the physical, psychological and social functioning of the individual. There is now a general consensus in the field for such a broad working definition for addictive behaviours (Gossop, 1989).

Donovan and Marlatt (1988) list common denominators of addictive behaviours that may seem very familiar to those who are used to a more specific definition of an addiction such as alcoholism.

- The individual choosing to maintain the addictive involvement even when other, more gratifying, sources of reinforcement are present.
- Dependence upon the behaviour or experience, on either a physiological or psychological level, that may lead to withdrawal distress when the individual is prevented from engaging in the behaviour.
- Increasing high need for a given experience or behaviour representing a form of tolerance.

- Perceiving the need for the experience or a powerfully strong desire in the form of 'craving' having both physiological and cognitive underpinnings, the strength of the craving being gauged by how willing the person is to sacrifice other sources of reward or well-being in life to continue to engage in the addictive behaviour.
- The power of the addictive experience promoting a tendency for rapid reinstatement of the behaviour pattern following a period of non-involvement with it.

Going through the list the reader will find that the descriptions apply equally well to an addiction involving chemicals, to gambling or to compulsive sexual behaviours.

Donovan and Marlatt's working definition of addictive behaviours is applicable to each of Orford's (1985) descriptions of the phenomenology of excessive drinking, gambling, drug taking, eating and sexuality, despite the seeming exclusiveness and diversity of these behaviours. The reader will also find that he or she could extend this list much further to include almost any human activity.

A common model of 'change'

Just as the study of addictions has come together in the past decade to the present phase of synthesis, similar processes have been taking place within disciplines too. Notably in psychology the seemingly opposite camps of behaviourism and psychodynamics have formed bridges. The emergence of social learning theory (Bandura, 1977) has played a major part in this process. Social learning theory gave rise to what is known as the cognitive revolution in psychology. In the clinical field it has led to the proliferation of cognitive behavioural therapies. A related development in the field of therapies is a growing sense of eclecticism. Holistic models of change that are a result of such developments (for example Prochaska and DiClementi 1983; Fig. 1.1) offer great hope for the shaping of psychological therapies for the future.

A model of behaviour change: Prochaska and DiClementi (1983)

The central concept in this model is that behaviour change takes place through a series of discrete stages. The 'precontemplation' stage is the period prior to the individual recognising the need to change. The next stage in the change process is the 'contemplation' stage where the person recognises the problem and considers doing some thing about

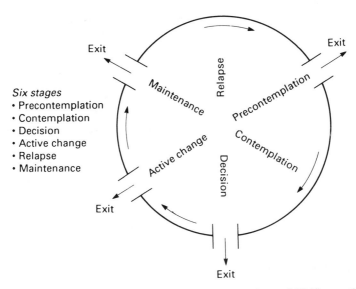

Fig. 1.1.   Revolving door model of change: Prochaska and DiClementi (1983).

it. It is possible for the individual to remain at this stage indefinitely if ambivalence to move on to the next stage is not resolved. The 'active change' stage is where the individual attempts to change behaviour by his or her own efforts or by seeking outside help (treatment). The final stage is the 'maintenance' stage where the individual struggles to maintain the changes made.

An important feature of this model is that it is a 'circular' model of change as opposed to a 'linear' one. This offers a more optimistic approach to behaviour change. If the person 'relapsed', he or she could re-enter the cycle and go through the process again until the desired outcome was reached (exits and re-entry points).

The implication of treatment matching is the most salient aspect of this model. Each phase may require a very specific therapeutic approach which may or may not be complementary to general counselling the client is receiving. For example if a client is in the 'precontemplation' phase, the therapeutic approach most suitable would be 'motivational interviewing' (Miller, 1983; 1985), whereas a 'client centred' type of counselling approach (Rogers, 1967) may not necessarily move the client on to doing something about his or her addiction.

Relapse prevention is clearly aimed at the 'maintenance phase' in the model. It is also aimed at getting a person back into the cycle following a relapse. Re-entry could be back into any phase. Relapse prevention aims to facilitate the process. This model enables a therapist to plan and match interventions with a definite sense of direction. Needless to say it also provides a framework to evaluate therapy and focus on particular areas when things go wrong.

What is relapse?

Relapse is described as the most common outcome of interventions with addictive behaviours. Mark Twain's much quoted remark about smoking – 'giving up smoking is easy, I've done it hundreds of times' – sums this up. The commonly used definition of relapse is a medical definition which describes it as the 'recurrence of symptoms of a disease after a period of improvement'.

Applying this black-and-white definition to addictions is problematic, even if one accepts all the assumptions of the medical/disease concept, because:

(1) Abstinence has to be the only goal. Whilst this may be a goal for interventions with substance abuse, it cannot be the goal across the range of addictive behaviours.
(2) Achievements of reduced (safe) levels of activity cannot be accommodated within this definition.
(3) It views relapse as a passive 'all or nothing' phenomenon. Research findings in the field of addictions point to relapse being a process rather than a single event phenomenon (Litman, 1980, Litman *et al.*, 1977, 1979, 1984; Marlatt and Gordon, 1980; Curry *et al.*, 1987).

From an 'addictive behaviours' perspective, the following working definition of relapse attempts to address some of the problems posed by a more traditional definition:

'Relapse can be viewed as a return to previous levels of activity following an attempt to stop or reduce that activity.'

Or alternatively:

'Relapse can simply be viewed as a failure to reach targets/goals set by the individual over a set period of time.'

This manual is based on the above working definitions of relapse which can be used for both 'abstinence' orientated and 'control' orientated interventions.

Lapse or relapse?

With the traditional definition of relapse, any 'lapse' or 'slip' is viewed as a switch which turns on a full blown relapse. This view of 'lapse =

relapse' takes away any potential for learning or corrective action. When the 'lapse = relapse' view becomes firmly engraved in a persons belief system it invariably acts as a self-fulfilling prophecy, e.g. 'one drink and a drunk'. It does not leave any margin for error.

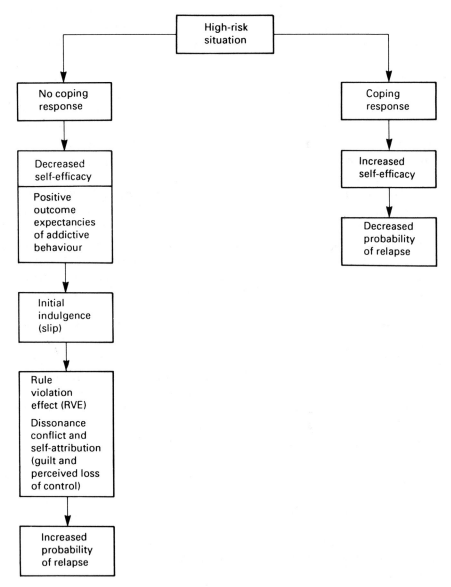

Fig. 1.2.   Cognitive/behavioural model of the relapse process, based on Marlatt and Gordon (1985).

Taking the view that a 'lapse' does not mean 'relapse', this manual adopts the following definition of a lapse:

> 'Any discrete violation of a self-imposed rule or a set of regulations governing the rate or pattern of a selected target behaviour.'

Preventing a slip or a lapse from becoming a full blown relapse is one of the main objectives of the relapse prevention programme. The relapse prevention approach to errors and slips is best summed up by the metaphor of a 'fire drill': to equip the person with a plan of action 'in case...'.

Relapse is viewed as not taking place as one event, like turning on a switch, but through a series of cognitive, behavioural and affective processes. A model of relapse based on such a view has been formulated by Marlatt and Gordon (1985) assimilating clinical experience and research findings spanning over a decade. The programme described in this manual uses this cognitive/behavioural model of relapse (Fig. 1.2) as its basis.

It is beyond the scope of this manual to discuss the background theory and research leading to its development. A reader interested in this is referred to the following publications: Marlatt and Gordon (1985; 1980); Cummings *et al.* (1980), Marlatt and Parkes (1982); and Marlatt (1978; 1982). The model is based on the assumption that it is largely psychological factors (thinking processes and mood) following a lapse that decide whether the person returns to the previous level of activity, i.e. relapse.

The reader is reminded that this model is directed at the 'maintenance' phase of behaviour change (Prochaska and DiClementi model). It is for those who have made a *choice* of *voluntary* control of their addictive behaviour. The client's decision could be either to abstain from the addictive behaviour or have clear targets of control. It is assumed that the client, while abstaining or keeping to his or her targets, experiences a sense of self-control (self-efficacy); the longer the person keeps to his or her targets, the greater the perception of self-efficacy (Bandura, 1977).

High-risk situation (HRS)

Research into the relapse process has shown that the primary obstacle that a person encounters in the maintenance phase is exposure to a *high-risk situation* (HRS) (Cummings *et al.*, 1980; Annis and Davis, 1988; Rist and Watzl, 1983).

A HRS can be defined as any situation or condition that poses a threat to the individual's sense of control (self-efficacy) and increases the risk of potential relapse. While these situations could be very specific to an individual, research shows that there are broad general categories of situations that are associated with high rates of relapse (Cummings *et al.*, 1980). These categories are briefly discussed here.

Intra-personal determinants

Negative emotional states

These are emotional states (moods and feelings) such as anger, frustration, anxiety, sadness, depression and boredom. They are conditions placed within the individual (intra-personal), feelings that were perhaps previously dealt with by indulging in the addictive behaviour. If this was the case the individual would have poor coping responses to deal with these states.

Positive emotional states

Therapists working in the field would be familiar with clients describing situations when they felt good, confident or like celebrating, and decided to indulge in the addictive behaviour. Although on the face of it this runs contrary to the self-efficacy argument, descriptions of emotional states and cognitive processes following such an event fit in well with Marlatt and Gordon's model of relapse.

Inter-personal determinants

Inter-personal conflict

The second highest rates of relapse in published studies are seen in this general category. These situations include conflicts with friends, marital partners, family members, co-workers, employers and employees.

Social pressure

Direct or indirect social pressure is another general situational category associated with high rates of relapse. An example of direct pressure would be a situation where an individual or group coerce or attempt to persuade an individual to indulge in the addictive behaviour. A situation of indirect pressure would be one in which the individual perceived a pressure to conform, perhaps by lighting a cigarette at a party because everyone else was smoking.

Coping response (yes/no?)

To a person trying to maintain a 'habit change', encountering high-risk situations is bound to be a constant hazard. Some of these situations may be avoidable but the majority may not be. Hence whether or not the person has the ability to cope with high-risk situations becomes a crucial factor in preventing relapse. 'Coping' is a key element in the relapse prevention model which has its foundations in health psychology and behavioural medicine. Together with increasing 'awareness' and 'lifestyle change', developing 'coping' responses forms the main goals of relapse prevention (Fig. 1.3).

There are two aspects of coping that are of relevance here.

(1) The individual having cognitive/behavioural skills to cope with specific high-risk situations.
(2) The individual having cognitive/behavioural skills to cope with stress (life stressors) in general which may or may not include the specific high-risk situations.

It may be that the person has used the addictive behaviour as the main coping response to deal with a whole range of stressors such as anxiety, conflict, depression, pain etc. If this was the case the person is more than likely to be weak or deficient in more adaptive coping responses (problem solving, being assertive). It is often found in problem drinkers or drug abusers with long histories that on cessation of

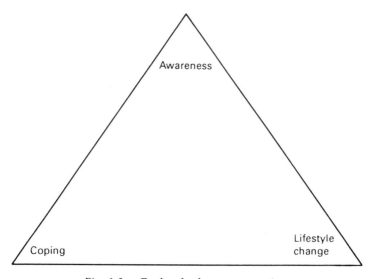

Fig. 1.3. Goals of relapse prevention.

the addictive behaviour, they find it extremely difficult to cope with even minimal stressors. Because of their addiction they have either failed to learn more adaptive coping responses or they have become de-skilled in using them.

The cognitive/behavioural model assumes having or not having coping response to be a major determinant of relapse. Thus identifying, learning and strengthening coping responses becomes a major goal in relapse prevention. They are dealt with as:

(1) Specific intervention strategies (e.g. skills training).
(2) Global intervention strategies (e.g. lifestyle change).

Decreased self-efficacy: positive outcome expectancies

Cognitive/behavioural formulations of 'coping' used in the model are closely linked to the concept of self-efficacy (Bandura, 1977). Efficacy expectations or confidence of being able to cope with high-risk situations have been shown to be predictive of relapse (Allsop and Saunders, 1989, Annis and Davis, 1988b; Colletti *et al.*, 1985; Condiotte and Lichtenstein, 1981). Helen Annis and her colleagues have developed a relapse prevention programme focusing on self-efficacy and high-risk situations alone (Annis and Davis, 1988). Assessment instruments focusing on efficacy expectations (for example the Situational Confidence Questionnaire for problem drinking, Annis, 1984) have proved to be invaluable in planning and carrying out interventions.

Studies on accounts of relapse of individuals with addictive problems have shown 'positive outcome expectancies' of the addictive behaviour to be a dominant cognitive factor at times of decreased self-efficacy (Marlatt and Rohsensow, 1980; Cooney *et al.*, 1987). A conflict is set up between the feelings of inadequacy (decreased self-efficacy) and the attractiveness of engaging in the addictive behaviour (dissonance conflict). The negative consequences of indulging in the addictive behaviour become largely ignored. If the person gives in at this stage a whole series of cognitive processes are likely to take place. These are dealt with in the next section.

Rule violation effect, dissonance conflict and self-attribution

Following a slip or initial indulgence in the addictive behaviour the model describes common thinking patterns that take place and that decide whether or not the person will proceed to have a full-blown relapse. This is considered to be a crucial stage in the relapse process.

The *rule violation effect* (RVE) (Marlatt, 1978; Marlatt and Gordon, 1980) is one such pattern of thinking. Paradoxically this pattern of thinking is one that is overtly promoted in traditional abstinence orientated (12-step) programmes (e.g. one drink and you are a drunk). Marlatt and Gordon (1985) argue that a strong belief and expectation of such a phenomenon make it a self-fulfilling prophecy, rather than any underlying physiological mechanism.

Dissonance conflict is another cognitive factor that is assumed to play a key role at this stage according to the model. Conflict arises from the individual's beliefs and expectancies about himself (e.g having control) and the indulgent behaviour (having a slip). According to cognitive dissonance theory (Festinger, 1964) the disparity between belief and behaviour would act to increase dissonance and the individual would be motivated to reduce dissonance by continuing to indulge and by reducing beliefs of control: 'I never had control, I might as well continue.' This according to the model greatly increases the probability of relapse.

In summary, the model describes a process whereby a combination of cognitive and behavioural factors could contribute to relapse in a series of discrete stages (see Fig. 1.4).

Covert antecedents of relapse

Marlatt and Gordon (1985) also propose a model that describe processes that could lead the individual to high-risk situations (Fig. 1.5). This can be looked upon as the pre-high-risk situation part of the overall model.

Lifestyle imbalance

This model proposes lifestyle imbalance as a fundamental factor in the relapse process. Lifestyle imbalance is described as the imbalance between activities associated with external pressure (shoulds) and the pleasurable activities the person does for him or herself (wants). The underlying assumption is that an individual's overall 'stress level' is closely associated with lifestyle imbalances which give rise to feelings of 'self-deprivation'. This is often used by individuals to justify indulgence ('I owe myself a cigarette, drink, etc.'), hence increasing the probability of relapse. Feelings of self-deprivation are also accumulated by some clients to produce the need for instant gratification (the 'final straw' phenomenon).

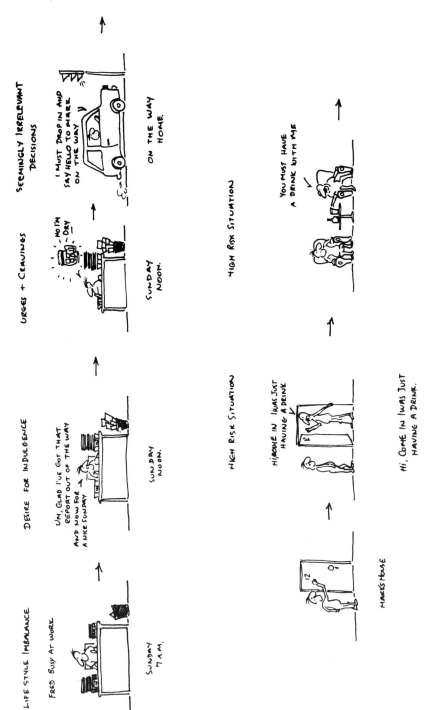

Fig. 1.4. To relapse or not to relapse!

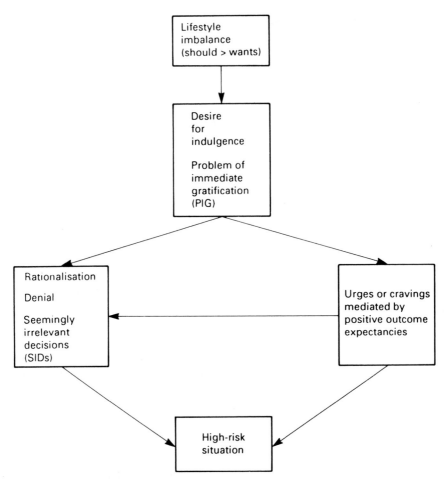

Fig. 1.5.   Correct antecedents in the relapse process, based on Marlatt and Gordon (1985).

Urges and cravings

An *urge* is defined as a relatively sudden impulse to engage in an act whereas a *craving* is the subjective desire to experience the effects or consequences of that act. According to the model when an individual who is having feelings of self deprivation because of the imbalance in his or her lifestyle, experience urges or cravings, the resolve to maintain behaviour change is threatened. If faced with a high-risk situation, the probability of relapse is increased.

Rationalisation and denial

It is proposed that cognitive factors also mediate at the stage when the individual is experiencing the desire to indulge. Rationalisation can be used at this stage to justify indulgence. This is when a person searches for a legitimate excuse to indulge.

Denial can also be used at this stage. Not accepting 'true' underlying reasons for behaviours and refusing to recognise selected aspects of a situation are examples of this. Rationalisation and denial are used in the model as defence mechanisms, as in psychodynamic theory. Rationalisation and denial help to reduce guilt and anxiety resulting from the decision to indulge.

Seemingly irrelevant decisions (SIDs)

Covert planning of relapse through a series of decisions is a key cognitive mediator that is proposed in this model. The pattern of making a series of mini decisions that brings a person to a high-risk situation that it would take a moral superhero to resist are called *seemingly irrelevant decisions* (SIDs). This process by which the individual 'set him or herself up' for relapse is described in more detail in Chapters 6 and 8.

Utility of the cognitive/behavioural model of relapse

For a therapist working in the field of addictions the relevance and possible utility of the model can be listed as follows:

- It is a model derived from research evidence.

- The model provides the therapist with a precise framework for proactive interventions. It enables the therapist to target and plan interventions systematically.

- It provides the therapist with a framework to analyse and understand a particular relapse episode of a client. Often therapists working in addictions experience feelings of frustration or despondency when faced with a client's relapse (perhaps repeated). If one adopts a concrete all-or-nothing approach to relapse this means the total destruction of all the hard work put in by the client and the therapist.

The cognitive/behavioural model enables the therapist to pinpoint where the client went wrong thus identifying weak areas that can be worked on. This inevitably adds a dimension of optimism for future interventions.

The therapist may also find that two relapse episodes in the same client may not be caused by the same factors. The model enables interventions to be carried out at different levels and at different points depending on a particular client's needs.

Application of the model

The above section outlined a cognitive/behavioural model of the 're-lapse process'. This section looks at what a therapist can do in planning and carrying out interventions in terms of the model.

The intervention strategies of the relapse prevention programme can be placed in the following broad categories:

- Assessment procedures.
- Insight/awareness increasing procedures.
- Skills training.
- Cognitive strategies.
- Lifestyle interventions.

These strategies are drawn from a wide area in cognitive and behavioural psychology and from more general schools of life change, such as Buddhist philosophy. This manual lists and describes a limited number of intervention strategies that would enable the reader to carry out an effective relapse prevention programme. Interventions included in the manual are a small portion in terms of the overall scope of the model. A good understanding of the model should enable the therapist to be creative and introduce interventions drawn from his or her own experience and background.

The interventions in the five categories listed above can be reclassified, according to the objectives of their use, into two groups:

(1) Specific intervention strategies
(2) Global intervention strategies.

Specific intervention strategies

These would include any intervention that is targeted towards a client's specific vulnerabilities or high-risk situations. These are interventions that are focused on immediate causes/events that point to relapse. For example, for a client with a drinking problem who has a tendency to relapse when under social pressure to drink, assertiveness skills training would be a specific intervention strategy. For a client who lights up a cigarette when feeling anxious or tense, teaching relaxation techniques would be a specific intervention strategy.

The aim of specific intervention strategies is to teach the client the skills of anticipating and coping with high-risk situations.

Global self-control strategies

These are strategies aimed at making general and global changes in the individual. This aspect of relapse prevention has its origins in health psychology and holistic medicine. The interventions included in this category range from interventions that are aimed at how a person approaches and solves problems to changing their whole lifestyle. Whereas 'specific interventions' aim towards developing mechanistic type responses (how to cope with a given high-risk situation), 'global interventions' aim at more general, deep-structured long-term change in the individual. The latter could include, for example, interventions to change attitude, lifestyle, diet, self-confidence and ways of interpreting situations.

From a therapist's point of view the category of 'global interventions' can include the whole spectrum of psychological therapies depending on the client's needs. This could range from problem solving therapy to long-term dynamic psychotherapy. If a therapist adopts a developmental model of change in addictions (Gorsky and Miller, 1983), a relapse prevention programme can be planned so that there is a progression from specific to global interventions. Gorsky and Miller (1983) within a disease framework propose a stage or phased model of recov-

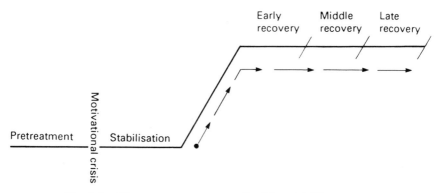

Fig. 1.6. The recovery process: Gorski and Miller (1983).

ery from addictions, each non-use stage representing a stage on the ladder. The overall adjustment the individual makes in recovery, taking place in the final phases in their model (see Fig. 1.6), includes the type of changes the 'global intervention' strategies of relapse prevention aim at.

In general, especially in short-term therapy, both specific and global interventions can be used concurrently in relapse prevention. As the reader would discover there is considerable overlap between the strategies and the distinction is often arbitrary. Some strategies, such as assertiveness training can be both a specific and global intervention. The dichotomy is only made so that the therapist would be clear in his or her mind and could communicate clearly to the client the overall aim of each intervention.

The big picture

An overview of relapse prevention intervention strategies included in this manual and their use in terms of Marlatt and Gordon's (1985) model of relapse is presented in Fig. 1.7. A brief description and rationale of the strategies is given below.

Assessment procedures

In cognitive behavioural therapies the distinction between assessment and intervention is sometimes arbitrary. Often focusing on behaviours and their controlling variables becomes a powerful therapeutic intervention (Miller, 1983). This is indeed the case in relapse prevention where many of the assessment procedures (e.g. self-monitoring) often prove to be very effective interventions.

Behavioural assessment

Behavioural assessment is the identification and measurement of behaviours and their controlling variables, for the purpose of understanding and altering them (Nelson and Hays, 1981). The main focus of assessment is what the person does rather than what the person has (Mischel, 1968).

Behavioural assessment in relapse prevention is mainly aimed at quantifying the addictive behaviour (the number of cigarettes, units of alcohol, etc., consumed per day), identifying high-risk situations (in-

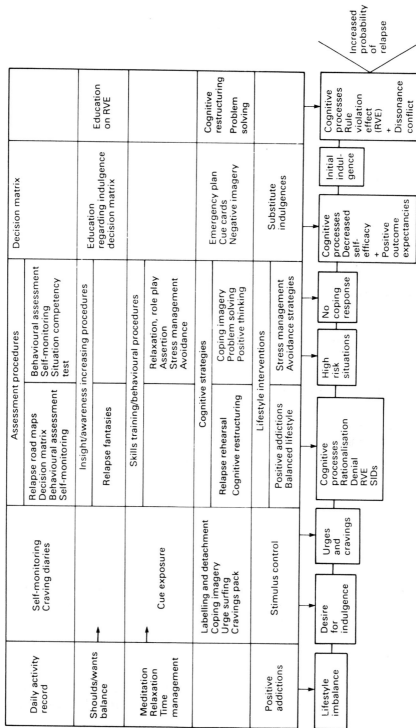

Fig. 1.7. Relapse prevention overview of model and interventions, based on Marlatt and Gordon (1985).

trapersonal, interpersonal, group pressure, etc.) and identifying coping skills and deficits. The 'stimulus (trigger) – organism (individual) – response (addictive behaviour and coping skills) – consequences' (SORC) framework (Goldfried and Sprafkin, 1976) forms the basis of behavioural assessment.

When do you use behavioural assessment?

In general behavioural assessment is used at the beginning of a relapse prevention programme. On the other hand assessment techniques such as self-monitoring (see the craving diary, Chapter 4) can be used throughout a programme. Depending on the individual client's needs and goals different behavioural assessment techniques may be appropriate at various stages of the programme.

What methods of behavioural assessment are used?

There are many different methods that can be used to carry out behavioural assessment. Assessment methods that could be used in a relapse prevention programme are listed below.

(1) *Direct observation.* This could be carried out in natural situations (observing a problem drinker in a pub, observing a smoker at a party) or in analogue situations (role-play). In analogue situations which afford the luxury of pre-planning and setting up, the use of a video camera is an invaluable aid. This enables close analysis of behaviour that is not possible otherwise.

(2) *Self monitoring.* This is the behavioural assessment technique which has the widest application in relapse prevention. For this reason it is described in more detail in the next section.

(3) *Interviews.* This is the most commonly used method of assessment. There are standardised interviews designed to collect information for behavioural assessment (SORC information) for various addictive behaviours. The reader is referred to recent texts such as Baker and Canon (1988) and Donovan and Marlatt (1988) for details of these procedures.

(4) *Role-play.* To find out whether or not a client has specific skills (e.g. assertive skills), role-play is a very useful assessment method. Role-play is most useful when the behaviour to be assessed is specified in detail, for example body posture when refusing a drink.

(5) *Questionnaires.* Questionnaires of various sort have wide applicability in relapse prevention. Again the reader is referred to Donovan and Marlatt (1988) and Baker and Canon (1988) for details of the range of questionnaires that could be used in relapse prevention.

Self-monitoring

This is one of the most simple and effective tools in behaviour therapy which could function both as an assessment method and as an intervention. Getting a person to keep a detailed record of an activity is all that it entails. When this is suggested to clients it is often met with a response of bemusement or indignation. A common response from clients who are uncomfortable or resistant to the idea is 'I can tell you now' followed by a description of their activities. Yet, once persuaded to do so, clients invariably return with very positive feedback with the exercise having considerable impact. With some clients the 'insight' gained from this intervention alone has proved sufficient to change behaviour.

As with all psychological interventions it is important that the therapist communicates the rationale behind the exercise effectively (sell the idea) to the client to achieve compliance. Having a clear idea of the objectives undoubtedly helps good communication. The objectives of self monitoring can be listed as follows:

- To get the client to consciously focus on the behaviour he or she wishes to change.
- To discover the behaviour or habit patterns (when, how and where).
- To identify possible triggers.
- To identify high-risk situations (low mood, conflict, social pressure, etc.).
- To identify the consequences of the behaviour to the individual/ people around them.
- To calculate the cost to the individual in physical, emotional and financial terms.

When to use self-monitoring

Self-monitoring can be used at any stage of the programme. If the treatment goal is control as opposed to abstinence self-monitoring should be continuous. In general self-monitoring is used most at the beginning of the programme and gradually discontinued as the individual regains control. In abstinence orientated programmes 'craving diaries' (see Chapter 4) are an example of self-monitoring that can be used throughout the programme.

An example

Drinking diaries are probably the most commonly used self-monitoring device in the addiction field. The example given here (see Appendix A(I) is designed to meet all of the objectives listed in the above section. Self-monitoring forms or diaries are easily designed. Therapists are advised to construct/design their own forms to cater for the particular addiction they are dealing with. Sometimes it may be necessary to design forms to meet the needs of a particular client.

Utility of self-monitoring

The primary use of self-monitoring in relapse prevention is to assess high-risk situations. Provided the client is totally compliant, self-monitoring also helps break down systems of denial and identify errors of thinking (cognitive distortions).

Negative addictions are are often described as bad habits, which carries the implication of being an automatic process. Addictive behaviours are sometimes carried out unthinkingly like driving a car or riding a bicycle. The metaphor of being on 'autopilot' describes this phenomenon. In certain situations or under certain conditions individuals seem to almost automatically slip into their addictive behaviour. A smoker reaching out for a cigarette under certain conditions is a good example of this. Clients often seem unaware of cues, triggers and patterns of their behaviour. Focusing on details of behaviour in this fashion often has the effect of 'jolting' the person out of 'autopilot'.

Another startling effect of self monitoring that we have often found is that of getting clients to calculate what the addictive behaviour costs them. This effect demonstrates how strong some clients' denial systems are.

Decision balance sheet (decision matrix)

This is simply a way of organising information to aid rational decision making. It provides a format where the pros and cons of an action (indulging in addictive behaviour) can be weighed up. Making clients aware of the decision process and teaching decision-making skills to those who are deficient forms an important part of the relapse prevention programme (see Chapter 8).

The decision matrix functions as a useful assessment tool as well as an intervention technique. For clients who are in an early stage of change in terms of the Prochaska and DiClementi model, the decision matrix is a very effective tool in moving them on to the next stage. Motivation for change will be dependent on the clients' perception of the positive and negative consequences of changing their behaviour. Writing positive and negative consequences down in the logical fashion of the decision matrix format not only helps clarify the issues but also helps to reinforce changes (the client carries a decision balance sheet at all times and refers to it when experiencing urges and cravings).

In our relapse prevention programme the 'decision balance sheet' is used extensively both as an assessment tool and as an intervention technique. Like other assessment instruments it is often useful for both the therapist and the client to have copies of the balance sheet.

Insight/awareness increasing procedures

Relapse road maps and description of past relapses
We have found using the metaphor of a journey and getting the client to describe past relapses or possible future relapses in a form of a map to be a very effective strategy. Clients are encouraged to identify possible future dangers (HRS) as destinations. They are also asked to identify 'early warning signs' that would indicate that they are heading towards their destination. The early warning signs are explored as decisional points where turning off to take an alternative route could be made. At each decisional point clients are advised to list the arguments against heading towards the destination.

This strategy can be used on a weekly basis where a client can plan the week ahead in terms of danger points.

These techniques could also be used towards the end of the programme when a client can be asked to describe alternative routes in terms of skills, techniques and strategies to avoid these destinations that have been learnt in the relapse prevention programme (see Chapter 11).

Relapse fantasies
Identifying and coping with high-risk situations were described as the main goals of relapse prevention. Getting clients to produce relapse fantasies is another useful technique to help achieve these goals.

In more traditional abstinence orientated programmes relapse is a subject that tends to be dealt with as the 'unspeakable' or the 'unthinkable'. Getting clients to produce a relapse fantasy is one technique that highlights the difference between relapse prevention and more traditional approaches. By using this technique from an assessment perspective the therapist could glean useful information about:

(1) High-risk situations.
(2) Specific vulnerabilities and coping skills.
(3) The client's self image and the role of the addictive behaviour in that image.

As an intervention strategy it invariably produces increased awareness in the client about his or her vulnerabilities and high-risk situations.

Skills training and behavioural procedures

Relaxation training

Anxiety often lies at the root of addictive behaviours and acts as a major factor in their maintenance. Tracing back the development of an addictive behaviour a therapist would invariably find an association of the addiction with anxiety. Many clients would not have learnt other coping responses or would have lost other coping skills, thus taking away the addictive behaviour would make them feel particularly vulnerable when faced with anxiety. For a person without coping skills everyday life stressors could become high-risk situations. Any of the general or specific high-risk situations may be anxiety provoking to the client.

Relaxation training is a tried and tested (Jacobson, 1976) strategy for coping with anxiety. There are many different techniques that can be used for relaxation training. Jacobson's progressive relaxation training is a method widely used in behaviour therapy and has lent itself to many adaptations. Our programme places great emphasis on relaxation training and recommends its use at the end of each session. Anxiety and its management are dealt with in more detail in Chapter 3.

Assertiveness training

Social skills deficits are often found in individuals with addictive problems and difficulties in assertive behaviour ranks on top (Chaney *et al.*, 1978; Foy *et al.*, 1976). In running relapse prevention programmes we recommend at least one session be devoted to assertiveness training. Details of assertiveness training are dealt with in Chapter 7.

Cue Exposure

Our clients have often reported that exposure to cues associated with their addictive behaviour has given rise to urges and craving that have lead to slips and subsequently to relapse. They report that exposure to cues has been particularly difficult in the early stages in the change process. For some, exposure to cues constitutes a major 'high risk'. This phenomenon of 'conditioned craving' has been described in the literature by a number of researchers (for example Seigel, 1983; O'Brien, 1976; O'Brien *et al.*, 1986). Marlatt and Gordon's (1985) model of relapse has been criticised for not placing due emphasis on this factor (Heather and Stallard, 1989).

Cue exposure is a counter conditioning procedure that can be used to deal with conditioned craving. This involves exposing the individual to stimuli associated with the addictive behaviour (desensitisation) under control conditions (such as in the presence of a therapist). The rationale behind this is that exposure to stimuli would result in adaptation/habituation. Riding out urges and cravings this way not only diminishes the effectiveness of the stimuli to trigger a response, but also helps increase the client's confidence (self-efficacy) of being able to resist the response.

Cue exposure can be adequately incorporated into a relapse prevention programme depending on the setting of therapy. It requires planning and time to carry out, hence it is best suited for individual work rather than work in the group mode. The therapist should ensure adequate debriefing (relaxation, meditation) following a cue exposure session. Exposure to cues involving alcohol (Rankin *et al.*, 1983; Cooney *et al.*, 1983;) and opiate use (O'Brien *et al.*, 1986) are examples of the use of cue exposure.

Other ways of dealing with conditioned craving are dealt with in Chapter 5.

Cognitive strategies

Cognitive restructuring
Relapse in addictive behaviours is often associated with 'errors in thinking' and typical patterns of thinking such as rule violation effect (RVE) and seemingly irrelevant decisions (SIDs). Identifying and changing these patterns of thinking and thinking errors form a major part of relapse prevention interventions. Chapters 5 and 6 deal with these issues in some depth.

Relapse rehearsal
Often clients have to make decisions and use coping skills in a state when they may have had a 'slip'. The rule violation effect (RVE) is likely to be the dominant cognitive process in such circumstances. Clients report that sometimes the skills learnt in an individual or group programme feel 'outside' the situation, external to the trance-like state they find themselves in. Relapse rehearsal is a useful technique which helps bridge the therapy'situation gap. This is a simple technique of

getting the client to imagine a situation where a slip has occurred and going through the decision process and possible coping skills that could be used. This technique is also a useful assessment tool as it helps the therapist and the client to identify deficits in decision making and coping skills. The procedure is dealt with in more detail in Chapter 10.

Labelling and detachment

Urges and cravings are phenomena with very specific qualities. They have a specific path, timing, intensity and duration. They don't last for ever. They come and go. Yet therapists may often find clients describe their experience of urges and cravings in terms of being passive victims of this terrible monster that grips them and won't let go.

If the therapist then questions the client on the path the experience takes, the client invariably gives clear information about triggers, latency of onset, intensity and duration. The therapist can use this information to point out to the client the cognitive errors (false beliefs, false assumptions and distortions in the interpretation of the experience) involved. The therapist should emphasise the fact that what ever the depth of intensity of the craving it will invariably 'pass away'.

Helping clients to reinterpret or 'reframe' their experience is an important part of the relapse prevention programme. Labelling and detachment are very effective ways of reframing the experience of urges and cravings.

The rationale is to teach the client to externalise (detach from) the experience. An effective way of doing this is to get the client to verbalise the experience in the third person, describing it as an observer instead of identifying with it and labelling the experience as would a dispassionate observer. Taking an example of a smoker, every time the client experiences a craving he or she would say to themselves 'X is experiencing a craving to smoke' instead of 'I am dying for a cigarette'.

This type of technique becomes after regular practice an automatic response and a structural or personal change. Hence it can be classed as a global intervention.

Also see Chapter 6.

Coping imagery

It was discussed earlier that 'coping' with high-risk situations, and more commonly with urges and cravings, would be a client's main objective in doing a relapse prevention programme. Teaching clients how to develop cognitive skills of 'coping' should feature high on the therapist's agenda. 'Coping' or 'efficacy-enhancing' imagery is one such cognitive skill.

The therapist may find that some clients can readily produce vivid imagery which is a great bonus. With others it may be very hard work. It is important to work out with the client imagery that he or she is comfortable with, can relate to and that has no 'hidden' connotations.

As with any other skill, practice is crucial for its effective development. Using the technique of guided fantasy (see Chapter 11) the therapist can get the client to practice coping imagery during the therapy session. In our experience this has proved to be a very effective method of teaching this skill.

Lifestyle interventions

Lifestyle balance
Marlatt and Gordon's (1985) model of relapse places unbalanced lifestyle as a fundamental factor in the relapse process.

The issue of lifestyle imbalance and ways of changing lifestyles are dealt with in more detail in Chapter 9.

Substitute indulgences
A substitute indulgence could be any activity that could provide immediate gratification and act as a diversion from indulging in the addictive behaviour. The therapist could work out with the client a list of activities that could be used when the client is experiencing a strong compulsion (urge, craving) to indulge in the negative addiction. If these activities can be built into the client's lifestyle it then becomes a global intervention. Having a deep bubbly bath when feeling an urge to drink instead of going to the pub can be taken as an example.

When substitute indulgences become part of the client's new lifestyle they can be used proactively in high-risk situations. The mere fact that the person has activities other than the addictive behaviour in his or her repertoire that give pleasure and gratification should act to reduce the probability of 'slips' or 'lapses' occurring.

The reader must also be warned about the danger of substitute indulgences themselves becoming negative addictions. When working out lists of substitute indulgences with clients the therapist must always be mindful about the probabilities of the activity being harmful in the long term. Avoiding 'addiction substitution' and 'addictive cycles' must receive careful consideration when using this strategy.

Positive addictions
It is often the case for many clients that the addictive behaviour has taken over much of their life or is extensively embedded into daily routine by the time they seek help. For such clients giving up or reducing the addictive behaviour means that they are left to cope with

an enormous vacuum in their lives. Many of our clients have described themselves as feeling like 'amputees' or having lost their 'best friend' without their addictive behaviour.

Relapse prevention deals with this issue via global strategies. The introduction of positive addictions is one such intervention. A 'positive addiction' is an obvious substitute for a 'negative addiction'. A positive addiction can be described as an activity that may or may not have immediate positive outcome but is beneficial to the individual in the long run. Positive addictions are dealt with in more detail in Chapter 9.

Stimulus control techniques

Physical and sensory properties of substances, places, situations and memories can all act as stimuli to trigger the response of a craving or an urge to indulge in the addictive behaviour. The smell of food, cigarette smoke, radio commentary of a race and the smells and sounds of a public bar are all examples of stimuli that can act to trigger strong urges and cravings in the addicted individual (see the section on cue exposure earlier in this chapter). Advertising exploits this phenomenon and could cause considerable distress to individuals trying to control some addictive behaviours.

In everyday life it is nearly impossible to avoid stimuli that trigger urges and cravings. Nevertheless it is possible to engineer environments to a certain extent to minimise exposure. Examples of this would be a problem drinker making sure that there is no alcohol lying around or within easy access in his or her environment, or a smoker changing old routines by having an alternative drink if coffee was associated with smoking. Stimulus control used in this sense is aimed at minimising exposure to stimuli associated with addictions and can be classified as a global intervention.

Considerations for clinical applications

When to use relapse prevention

It was discussed above that relapse prevention is clearly aimed at the 'maintenance' phase of habit change. This phase is preceded by either an initial phase of treatment or a clear decision about change and goals.

For addictions such as drug and alcohol misuse, the premaintenance or initial phase of treatment may involve 'detoxification' in an inpatient or community setting. In general the initial phase of treatment for addictions may include intensive psychological therapy or assessment (for example, motivational interviewing). An intensive initial phase of treatment is particularly applicable when the treatment goal is 'abstinence'. The intense initial treatment would focus on the immediate physiological and psychological consequences of 'withdrawal'. This may involve chemical and psychological interventions to deal with physical discomfort and acute anxiety (withdrawal distress) associated with the cessation of the addictive behaviour.

Relapse rates are generally found to be highest soon after or within a short period following the initial treatment/intervention phase (Hunt *et al.*, 1971). Hence relapse prevention is best directed towards the end of the initial phase.

The timing of commencement of relapse prevention would be entirely different for 'control' orientated interventions. For clients embarking on a *control path* relapse prevention is applicable soon after the decision phase of the changes process. A client could begin a relapse prevention programme from the time he or she sets the goals of change (the number of cigarettes, units of alcohol, etc.).

Other times when a relapse prevention programme may be appropriate for a client may be when the client has had a 'slip' after a period of successful maintenance. It is also appropriate for clients who go through a group programme to repeat the programme periodically, for example at three-monthly or six-monthly intervals.

For clients who have completed a programme we recommend regular follow-up sessions and top-up sessions. This could play a vital part in deciding the outcome (see the section on evaluation later in this chapter).

Group or individual programmes?

This manual describes a programme and a structure for use in a group setting. Although it teaches therapists to run groups, the entire programme can be translated into individual client work. For both individual and group work the therapist may decide to use the whole or part of the programme described here, depending on the needs and expectations of clients.

There may be advantages and disadvantages in the two approaches. Sometimes the therapist may find it appropriate to use both modes. For a client going into a group we strongly recommend a pre-group individual session to explain the programme and work out the client's expectations and anxieties (see Chapter 2). In our experience the pre-group individual sessions especially focusing on clients' anxieties and expectations have significantly reduced dropout rates from the programme (Keaney *et al.*, 1990: in preparation).

Although we don't feel seeing clients individually during a group programme is particularly productive, we have found individual follow-up sessions very useful. The latter give clients the chance to consolidate and make personal adaptations of skills, techniques and insights gained during the programme.

Settings for relapse prevention programmes

The programme described in this manual is based on groups that were run in out-patient and community settings. Relapse prevention groups can be run in any setting – in-patient, hostel, convalescent houses, day centres, day hospitals, private clinics etc. Individual relapse prevention sessions could be carried out with both in-patients and out-patients.

Evaluation of therapy

Evaluation is the assessment of the effectiveness of an intervention or treatment. In the present context evaluation would mean measuring the outcome of relapse prevention interventions. Evaluation is an essential component of any cognitive behavioural intervention. It has its applications both at the microscopic (individual interventions) and macroscopic (overall programme) levels.

It is important that the therapist keeps evaluation in mind when assessing a client. If appropriate and relevant information is not gathered at the initial assessment stage subsequent evaluation becomes impossible if not meaningless. Hence *evaluation criteria* have to be decided in advance of the initial assessment of the client for the programme so that this information can be collected. For therapists requiring more information on assessment we recommend recent texts by Donovan and Marlatt (1988) and Baker and Cannon (1988).

There are two aspects of evaluation that are relevant here:

(1) The client's satisfaction with the programme.
(2) The effectiveness of the programme in producing and maintaining change (outcome).

Although these aspects are dealt with separately it does not mean that they are mutually exclusive.

Satisfaction (impact)

This can be measured at the end of the programme, or after each session. We favour the latter because it also enables the measurement of the *impact* of the therapy session (Stiles, 1980). If the therapist opts to do session by session evaluation, both impact and satisfaction can be measured by a simple questionnaire (see Appendix A (III) for example). This information can provide the therapist with feed-back that can be helpful in different ways. Primarily it can provide the therapist with some indication of the effectiveness of therapy delivery (how well the message is getting through). It can also indicate the receptiveness of the individual client (how well the client is receiving the message). This information can be used to maximise the impact/effectiveness of the programme by making ongoing adjustments and client-specific interventions (discussions with the client about particular blocks and problems).

Drawbacks and problems of this type of evaluation must also be discussed here. If relapse prevention is carried out in a group format the most reliable feedback is obtained if the questionnaires are filled out anonymously. This of course does not allow for client-specific adjustments or interventions. On the other hand, if the questionnaires are used after individual sessions or not filled out anonymously after group sessions, social desirability factors (client not wanting to disappoint the therapist) could influence the reliability of the feedback.

For practical reasons the therapist may decide to evaluate the programme for client satisfaction only at the end of the programme. Examples of evaluation forms are given in Appendix A (IV); these can be modified to suite any a particular programme.

Programme effectiveness (outcome)

The question that is asked of all therapy programmes is how effective they are. What proportion of those going through the programme change their behaviour, what proportion maintain their change, and how many relapse and after what period are other questions that are frequently asked. For therapists working in the field of addictions these are not questions that are always welcome.

Traditionally the outcomes of addiction treatment programmes were measured by *rates of relapse* in six-month, one-year, 18-month and two-year follow-ups. The only outcome criterion was that of abstinence. Outcome was generally expressed in terms of rates of relapse (50 per cent, 80 per cent, etc.). The criterion used fitted in with the all-or-nothing, black-or-white disease concept based definition of relapse discussed earlier in this chapter.

Measuring outcome of a 'global' or 'holistic' programme such as relapse prevention in traditional 'black-or-white' terms is arguably meaningless. Acknowledging possible criticisms of 'moving the goal

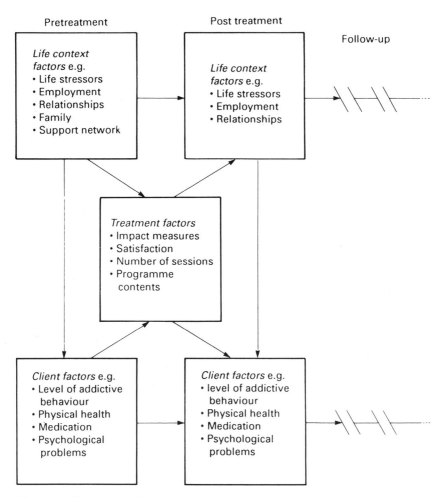

Fig. 1.8. Framework for evaluating treatment, based on Moos and Finney (1983).

post', while keeping the *level of addictive behaviour* as the *primary* measure of outcome we favour a more global outcome evaluation, taking factors such as mental and physical health, employment and family and social relationships into consideration.

The proposed evaluative framework (Fig. 1.8) is based on the process orientated framework for evaluation of alcohol treatment proposed by Moos and Finney (1983). The framework suggests a pre-treatment and post-treatment comparison of personal and life context factors of the client, linking them with aspects of treatment (components of the programme, measures of satisfaction). The same comparisons can be made at follow-up.

Personal and life context factors

The use of a standard questionnaire such as the addiction severity index (ASI) (McLellan *et al*. 1980; see Appendix A(V) should yield most of the information that would be needed in this area.

In instances where it is inappropriate or such an instrument is not available, the therapist could gather the appropriate information by asking specific questions during the assessment interview on, for example:

(1) History and current level of addictive behaviour.
(2) History and current state of physical health.
(3) History and current state of mental health (psychiatric and psychological problems).
(4) Current life stressors.
(5) Current support system, e.g. number of social contacts.
(6) Family and interpersonal relationships, e.g. marital conflict.
(7) Employment status.
(8) Legal problems.
(9) Other addictive behaviours.
(10) Demographic details.

These questions could then be repeated at the end of the programme and at follow-up. It is of course easier to administer a standard questionnaire such as the ASI which could then be repeated.

The therapist may decide to focus on very specific areas and devise a simple questionnaire that could then be repeated.

Another very simple and effective method of global evaluation is that of *problem listing*. This is done by asking the client to list three or four of what he or she considers the main problems in their life context in a descending order of severity on a sheet provided for this purpose. The client is then asked to rate the severity of each problem in a 0–10 scale or a visual analogue scale (see Appendix A(VI)). The same form or a new blank could be presented to the client at the end of the programme and at follow-up and the same procedure repeated.

The above method enables more global assessment of change. If new blanks are used at each stage of assessment the therapist may find that clients put down different problems or change the order of importance of the problems as well as giving different severity ratings.

It is extremely difficult to carry out evaluations with strict methodological criteria similar to drug trials (random allocations, placebo, double blind, etc.) in clinical settings for treatment of addictive problems because of ethical and practical considerations. Readers wishing to explore theoretical and methodological issues regarding the evaluation of addiction treatment programmes are referred to reviews by Cady (1980), Donovan (1988) and Maisto and Connors (1988).

Follow-up

Follow-up plays an important part in the treatment of addictions. It is not always possible to draw a clear distinction between what is considered treatment and what could be considered to be follow-up. The latter has been found to have a direct effect on outcome (Cady, 1980). The time of follow-up has also been found to influence the outcome rates (Emerick and Henson, 1983). It has been found that, on average, the longer after treatment the data are collected, the lower are the rates of improvement (Emerick 1982).

Follow-up for evaluation or as part of treatment?

In our experience follow-up has an important effect on maintenance and we recommend that it be included as part of the programme. There is evidence that points to a direct relationship between maintenance of change and maintenance of contact with the therapist (Janis, 1983). When giving clients an outline of the programme for a group or for structured individual sessions, the therapist should also discuss follow-up and where appropriate give appointments.

Follow-up could serve three functions:

(1) To give clients a structure/reference point to report back their progress.
(2) To function as top-up or refresher sessions for relapse prevention material.
(3) To enable data collection for evaluation of the programme.

It is left for the therapist to decide which of these functions follow-up sessions would serve. It is our experience that with sufficient advance planning it is possible to incorporate all three of the above functions into a follow-up session.

Frequency of follow-up

In general we recommend intervals of one month, three months and six months, with six-monthly follow-ups from then on. It is quite straightforward to do this for groups. When relapse prevention is carried out in the individual modality it is much more difficult to have such clearly marked out follow-up periods. Such difficulties arise because to a large extent the client may dictate frequency of sessions and follow-up. In the individual modality it may also be difficult to distinguish between treatment and follow-up.

For evaluation purposes the minimal follow-up periods recommended are 12 to 18 months (Moos *et al.*, 1982; Sobell *et al.*, 1980). Claims for effectiveness of treatment with shorter follow-up periods holds very little credibility.

References

Alden, L. (1980) 'Preventive Strategies in the Treatment of Alcohol Abuse: A Review and a Proposal'. In P. Davidson (Ed) *Behavioural Medicine: Changing Health Lifestyles*. Brunner/Mazel, New York.

Allsop, S. and Saunders, W. (1989) 'Relapse and alcohol problems'. In M. Gossop (Ed) *Relapse and Addictive Behaviour*. Tavistock/Routledge, London.

Annis, H.M. (1984) Situational Confidence Questionnaire, short form. Addiction Research Foundation, Toronto.

Annis, H.M. and Davis, C.S. (1988) 'Assessment of Expectancies'. In D.M. Donovan and G.A. Marlatt (Eds) *Assessment of Addictive Behaviours*. Guilford Press, New York.

Annis, H.M. and Davis, C.S. (1988b) 'Relapse Prevention'. In R.K. Hester and W.R. Miller (Eds) *Handbook of Alcoholism Treatment Approaches*. Pergamon Press, Inc., New York.

Baker, T.B. and Cannon, D.S. (Eds) (1988) *Assessment and Treatment of Addictive Disorders*. Praeger, New York.

Bandura, A. (1977) 'Self-efficacy: Towards a unifying theory of behavioral change'. *Psychological Review*, **84**, 191–215.

Baer, J.S. *et al.* (1988) 'Secondary prevention of alcohol abuse with college student populations: a skills-training approach'. In press.

Blane, H.T. (1976) 'Education and Prevention of Alcoholism.' In B. Kissin and H. Begleiter (Eds) *The biology of alcoholism, vol. IV*. Plenum, New York.

Brownell, K.D. *et al.* (1986). 'Understanding and Preventing Relapse.' *American Psychologist*, **41**, No. 7, 765–782.

Cady, G.R. (1980) 'A Review of problems in conducting alcohol treatment outcome studies'. In L.C. Sobell, M.B. Sobell and E. Ward (Eds) *Evaluating alcohol and drug abuse treatment effectiveness: Recent advances*. Pergamon Press, New York.

Chaney, E.F., O'Leary, M.R. and Marlatt, G.A. (1978) 'Skills training with alcoholics.' *Journal of Consulting and Clinical Psychology*, **46**, 1092–1104.

Colletti, G., Supnick, J.A. and Payne, T.J. (1985) 'The Smoking Self-Efficacy

Questionnaire (SSEQ): preliminary scale development and validation'. *Behavioural Assessment.* **7**: 249–60.

Condiotte, M.M. and Lichtenstein, E. (1981) 'Self-efficacy and relapse in smoking cessation programs'. *Journal of Consulting and Clinical Psychology.* **49**, 648–658.

Cooney, N.L., Baker, L.H. and Pomerleau, O.F. (1983) 'Cue exposure for relapse prevention in alcohol treatment'. In R.J. McMahon and K.D. Craig (Eds) *Advances in Clinical Behavior Therapy.* Brunner/Mazel, New York.

Cooney, N.L. *et al.* (1987) 'Cognitive changes after alcohol cue exposure'. *Journal of Consulting and Clinical Psychology,* **55**, 150–155.

Cummings, C., Gordon, J. and Marlatt, G.A. (1980) 'Relapse: prevention and prediction'. In W.R. Miller (Ed) *The Addictive Behaviors.* Pergamon, New York.

Curry, S., Marlatt, G.A. and Gordon, J.R. (1987) 'Abstinence Violation Effect: validation of an attributional construct with smoking cessation'. *Journal of Consulting and Clinical Psychology,* **55**: 145–149.

Donovan, D.M. (1988) 'Assessment of Addictive Behaviors, Implications of an Emerging Biopsychosocial Model'. In D.M. Donovan and G.A. Marlatt (Eds) *Assessment of Addictive Behaviors.* Guilford Press, New York.

Donovan, D.M. and Marlatt, G.A. (1988) *Assessment of Addictive Behaviors.* Guilford Press, New York.

Emerick, C.D. (1982) 'Evaluation of alcoholism psychotherapy methods.' In E.M. Pattison and E. Kaufman (Eds) *Encyclopedic handbook of alcoholism.* Gardner Press, New York.

Emerick, C.D. and Hanson, J. (1983) 'Assertions Regarding Effectiveness of Treatment of Alcoholism: Fact or Fantasy?'. *American Psychologist,* 1078–1088.

Festinger, L. (1964) *Conflict, decision and dissonance.* Stanford University Press, Stanford.

Foy, D.W. *et al.* (1976) 'Social skills training to teach alcoholics to refuse drinks effectively.' *Journal of Studies on Alcohol,* **37**, 1340–1345.

Goldfried, M.R. and Sprafkin, N.J. (1974) *Behavioral Personality Assessment.* General Learning Press, Morristown, N.J.

Goodwin, D.W. (1985) 'Alcoholism and Genetics: The Sins of the Fathers'. *Archives of General Psychiatry,* **42**, 171–174.

Gorsky, T.T. and Miller, M. (1983) *Staying Sober – A Guide to Relapse Prevention.* Alcoholism Systems Associates, Hazel Creste, Ill.

Gossop, M. (1989) *Relapse and Addictive Behaviour.* Tavistock/Routledge, London.

Heather, N. and Robertson, I. (1981) *Controlled drinking.* Methuen, London.

Heather, N. and Stallard, A. (1989) 'Does the Marlatt model underestimate the importance of conditioned craving in the relapse process?'. In M. Gossop (Ed) *Relapse and Addictive Behaviour.* Tavistock/Routledge, London.

Hunt, W.A., Barnett, L.W. and Branch, L.G. (1971) 'Relapse rates in addiction programs.' *Journal of Clinical Psychology,* **27**, 455–456

Jacobson, E. (1976) *You Must Relax.* Souvenir Press, London.

Janis, I.L. (1983) 'The Role of Social Support in Adherence to Stressful Decisions.' *American Psychologist,* 143–160.

Jellineck, E.M. (1960) *The disease concept of alcoholism*. Hillhouse Press, New Brunswick, N.J.

Kalb, M. (1975) 'The myth of alcoholism prevention.' *Preventive Medicine*, **4**, 404–416.

Keaney, F. *et al.* (1990) (in preparation). 'Community Based Relapse Prevention Programmes: The problem of drop-outs'. APAS, National Temperence Hospital, London.

Litman, G.K., Eiser, J.R. and Taylor, C. (1979) 'Dependence, relapse and extinction. A theoretical critique and behavioural examination.' *Journal of Clinical Psychology*, **35**, 192–199.

Litman, G.K. *et al.* (1984) 'The relationship between coping behaviours, their effectiveness and alcoholism relapse and survival'. *British Journal of Addiction*, **79**, 283–291.

Litman, G.K. *et al.* (1977) 'Towards a typology of relapse: a preliminary report'. *Drug and Alcohol Dependence*, **2**, 157–162.

Litman, G.K. (1980) 'Relapse in alcoholism: traditional and current approaches'. In G. Edwards and M. Grant (Eds) *Alcoholism: Treatment in Transition*. Croom Helm, London.

Maisto, S.A. and Connors, G.J. (1988) 'Assessment of Treatment Outcome'. In D.M. Donovan and G.A. Marlatt (Eds) *Assessment of Addictive Behaviors*. Guilford Press, New York.

Marlatt, G.A. and Gordon, J.R. (1985) *Relapse Prevention: Maintenance Strategies in the Treatment of Addictive Behaviors*. Guilford Press, New York.

Marlatt, G.A. (1978) 'Craving for alcohol, loss of control, and relapse: A cognitive-behavioural analysis.' In P.E. Nathan, G.A. Marlatt and T. Loberg (Eds) *Alcoholism: New directions in behavioral research and treatment*. Plenum, New York.

Marlatt, G.A. and Rohsensow, D.J. (1980) 'Cognitive processes in alcohol use: Expectancy and the balanced placebo design'. In N.K. Mello (Ed) *Advances in substance abuse* (Vol. 1). JAI Press, Greenwich, Conn.

Marlatt, G.A. (1982) 'Relapse prevention: A self-control program for the treatment of addictive behaviours'. In R.B. Stuart (Ed) *Adherence, compliance, and generalization in behavioral medicine*. Brunner/Mazel, New York.

Marlatt, G.A. and Gordon, G.A. (1989) 'Relapse Prevention: future directions'. In M. Gossop (Ed) *Relapse and Addictive Behaviour*. Tavistock/Routledge, London.

Marlatt, G.A. and Parks, G.A. (1982) 'Self-management in addictive disorders.' In P. Karoly and F.H. Kanfer (Eds) *Self-management and behavior change*. Pergamon Press, Elmsford, New York.

Marlatt, G.A. and Gordon, J.R. (1980) 'Determinants of relapse: Implications for the maintenance of behavior change.' In P.O. Davidson and S.M. Davidson (Eds) *Behavioral medicine: Changing health lifestyles*. Brunner/Mazel, New York.

McLellen, A.T., Luborsky, L. and Erdlen, F. (1980) 'The addiction severity index.' In E. Goltheil, A.T. McLellan and K.A. Druley (Eds) *Substance abuse and psychiatric illness*. Pergamon Press, New York.

Miller, W.R. (1985) 'Motivation for treatment: a review with special emphasis on alcoholism'. *Psychological Bulletin* **98**, 84–107.

Miller, W.R. (1983) 'Motivational interviewing with problem drinkers'. *Behavioural Psychotherapy*, **11**, 147–172.

Mischel, W. (1968) *Personality and assessment.* Wiley, New York.

Moos, R.H. and Finney, J.W. (1983) 'The Expanding Scope of Alcoholism Treatment Evaluation'. *American Psychologist*, 1036–1044.

Moos, R.H., Cronkite, R.C. and Finney, J.W. (1982) 'A conceptual framework for alcoholism treatment evaluation.' In E.M. Pattison and E. Kaufman (Eds) *Encyclopedic handbook of alcoholism.* Gardner Press, New York.

Nelson, R.O. and Hays, S.C. (1981) 'Nature of Behavioral Assessment'. In M. Hersen and A.S. Bellack (Eds) *Behavioral Assessment: a practical handbook.* Pergamon Press, New York.

O'Brien, C.P. (1976) 'Experimental analysis of conditioning factors in human narcotic addiction'. *Pharmacological Review*, **27**, 533–543.

O'Brien, C.P., Ehrman, R.N. and Ternes, J.W. (1986) 'Classical conditioning in human opioid dependence.' In S.R. Goldberg and I.P. Stolerman (Eds) *Behavioral Analysis of Drug Dependence.* Academic Press, New York.

Orford, J. (1985) *Excessive Appetites: A Psychological View of Addictions.* Wiley, Chichester.

Peel, S. (1985) *The meaning of addiction: A compulsive experience and its interpretation.* Lexington Books, Lexington, MA.

Prochaska, D.O. and DiClementi, C.C. (1983) 'Stages and processes of self-change of smoking: Towards an integrative model of change.' *Journal of Consulting and Clinical Psychology*, **51**, 390–395.

Rankin, H., Hodgson, R. and Stockwell, T. (1983) 'Cue exposure and response prevention with alcoholics: a controlled trial'. *Behaviour Research and Therapy*, **21**, 435–446.

Rist, F. and Watzl, H. (1983) 'Self assessment of relapse risk and assertiveness in relation to treatment outcome of female alcoholics.' *Addictive Behaviours*, **8**, 121–127.

Roffman, R.A., Gordon, J.R. and Craver, J.A. (1988) 'AIDS Risk Reduction: Preventing Relapse to Unsafe Sex' (unpublished manuscript). University of Washington.

Rogers, C.R. (1967) *On becoming a Person: A therapist's view of psychotherapy.* Constable, London.

Schuckit, M.A. (1987) 'Biological Vulnerability to Alcoholism.' *Journal of Consulting and Clinical Psychology*, **55**, No. 3, 301–309.

Seigel, S. (1983) 'Classical conditioning, drug tolerance and drug dependence'. In Y. Israel *et al.* (Eds) *Research Advances in Alcohol and Drug Problems.* Plenum, New York.

Shaffer, H.J. and Milkman, H.B. (1985) 'Crisis and conflict in the addictions'. In H.B. Milkman and H.J. Shaffer (Eds) *The addictions: Multidisciplinary perspective and treatments.* Lexington Books, Lexington, MA.

Sobel, M.B. and Sobel, L.C. (1978) *Behavioral treatment of alcohol problems.* Plenum, New York.

Sobel, M.B. *et al.* (1980) 'Developing a prototype for evaluating alcohol treatment effectiveness.' In L.C. Sobell, M.B. Sobell and E. Ward (Eds) *Evaluating alcohol and drug abuse treatment effectiveness: Recent advances.* Pergamon Press, New York.

Stiles, W.B. (1980) 'Measurement of the impact of psychotherapy sessions.' *Journal of Consulting and Clinical Psychology,* **48**, 176–185.

Chapter 2

Getting Started

Welcome to relapse prevention. Essentially, when working with addictions, the interventions that move a client into a change are different from those that maintain that change. In this chapter and the subsequent ones, we look very closely at interventions that maintain change.

This chapter is divided into three parts. The first part deals with the practical considerations for therapists starting a relapse prevention group. The second part deals with the assessment interview and the third with the first group.

Preparing the ground

Who does the group?

The best combination we found was a male and female therapist. Many of our groups had more male clients than female in a ratio of three to one. This may be different in other settings.

Goals of the therapists

(1) Reduce the number and severity of relapses.
(2) Our role primarily is to be professional communicators; to transmit certain concepts of the relapse prevention model to our clients.
(3) We wished to engage and retain our clients in treatment appropriately.

(4) Increase our clients' awareness of relapse issues (overlaps with goal (1)).

(5) To identify and challenge the cognitive errors of our clients (the thoughts and beliefs which hinder maintenance).

(6) We want clients to become their own therapist or maintenance agent (Annis and Davis, 1988). Our relationship is a co-operative one.

(7) For us as therapists we wanted the relapse prevention programme to be a positive learning experience that would contribute to our own growth and development.

Time commitments

The therapists should be prepared to commit time for the following:

- Three hours weekly for the groups for a period of six to eight weeks (group itself ran for two hours).
- Time for a follow-up group (if one is planned).
- A weekly pregroup therapists' planning session (usually half an hour).
- A weekly post group therapists' debriefing session (usually half an hour). These two groups are in addition to the weekly group.
- In our unit we also had a fortnightly supervision group (one hour) with a supervisor familiar with relapse prevention but not involved in our current group.
- A block of time for the assessment interviews (half an hour per interview).
- A shared commitment with the co-therapist to run a relapse prevention helpline (this is optional): While the group runs during office hours, if a client has problems he or she can contact you in an emergency. For example, a client in the group has a slip midway through and phones the helpline for advice or has a worry about an unanticipated high-risk situation outside of group time. In reality most clients made very little use of this service but it is a valuable back-up to them.
- Liaise with other workers. Write up handouts. Write up groups.

Number of clients in group

We found that a comfortable number to work with was between eight and ten; on average we had seven clients. We set an upper limit of twelve.

Tools of the Trade

- *Group room.*   The more comfortable the room, the better. A reasonably large room with good lighting is required especially if you are using a video camera to record events.
- *Kitchen and toilets.*   It is helpful to have tea and coffee facilities close by, and toilets.
- *Photocopying facilities.*   Because of handouts we found a photocopier invaluable.
- *Other materials.*   A flipchart was in constant use throughout each group, we found our word processor a treasure for updating our handouts as the groups evolved, and lastly a locked filing cabinet with a member of our team taking responsibility for updating our records. We had the services of a committed and excellent secretary.

Attracting customers

Over the years of running relapse prevention groups, it was our impression that most clients who enter a treatment programme can benefit from the relapse prevention model. We supplied our colleagues with an information sheet that we were starting a group. For some groups we left information flyers in the reception area. In addition we left a referral book available so our colleagues could write in possible attenders well in advance. Figure 2.1 shows an example of the information sheet for colleagues while Fig. 2.2 shows a typical information leaflet.

RELAPSE PREVENTION GROUP

Starts Tuesday 30 January 1990 and continues on Tuesday 6, 13, 20, 27 February and 27 March. Follow-up group Tuesday 10 April.

Time 9.00 AM for 9.15 AM. Coffee, tea available at 9.00 AM in the new ground floor group room. Group finishes at 11.15 AM

Assessment interviews will be held on Tuesday 23 January. Contact our secretary for appointments.

An information sheet for attenders will be available on Tuesday 16 January 1990.

Fig. 2.1.   Example of an information sheet for colleagues.

CHANGING PERSONAL SEXUAL PRACTICE

A GROUP FOR GAY MEN

DO you find it a struggle to
maintain safer sex?

HAS unsafe sex become
addictive?

DO you feel under pressure,
unhappy, confused
about your behaviour?

IF you have a problem and
want to discuss ways of
changing

PLEASE READ ON......

This group will be based on a way of working called "relapse prevention", in which we look at how to change behaviour and how to maintain that change.

We will focus on a range of issues including:

- setting personal sexual goals
- achieving important balances in lifestyle
- identifying high risk situations
- improving coping skills and self-esteem
- taking on the challenge of safer sex practice
- general information on sexually transmitted diseases
- managing stress and anxiety

The content of the course will include use of group discussion, self-monitoring diary, relaxation techniques and new video work on safer sex.

NOTE: This is a group for gay men irrespective of HIV positive status.

Fig. 2.2.   Example of an information leaflet.

Setting up the assessment interview

Once you have confirmed your dates for the group we advise that you have the assessment interviews fairly close to the starting date, preferably within fourteen days prior to starting.

We had left an appointment book with empty slots with our secretary so the key worker could give the client an assessment appointment. We also wrote to the client – see Fig. 2.3.

Unit Telephone Number
Address

Dear Christine,
Your relapse prevention assessment appointment is on Tuesday 24 January at 10.00 AM. The interview will last for half an hour. If you are unable to attend, please let us know. We look forward to meeting you.

Signed – Therapists.

Fig. 2.3.   An assessment appointment.

The assessment interview

Background to the assessment interview

In the three-and-a-half years of running relapse prevention groups, the attendance rate has varied. Some groups were quite well attended with a low dropout rate; others had one or two individuals drop out throughout the duration of the group. We were interested in why this might be and asked ourselves the following questions:

(1) What were we doing that was making some groups more successful than others?
(2) What made the difference?
(3) How can we incorporate these differences into running the programme?

When we first started doing groups we had a short pregroup interview. The interviews were informal, not very specific and much more about us giving information on what the groups were about than finding out what the needs of the clients were.

Following evaluation of the assessment interviews we have arrived at the current format which we use. The changes we made included:

(1) Having a greater awareness of the clients' needs.
(2) Having a clear structure.
(3) Being more specific.

The results have proven very positive and interesting. We now have a well-structured half-hour interview. It has resulted in some groups having just one person drop out and in one group nobody dropped out.

Screening for the client's suitability

Most clients attending a treatment programme/counselling agency are suitable for the relapse prevention programme, on either an individual or group basis. We currently work in a community setting but the relapse prevention programme can be adapted for in-patient, residential and other treatment locations.

We have found very few contraindications to a client participating in a relapse prevention programme. It is important to have the ability to communicate. For example, a client with severe depression may not be interested in expressing him or herself, whereas a client with a physical handicap, such as partial deafness, may have difficulties in receiving information. The use of flipcharts and handouts makes it desirable for a client to have reading and writing skills. Clients attending a group stoned or intoxicated were asked to leave (see notes section on ground rules).

We have had interesting debates about mixing clients who are aiming for abstinence and controlled drinking. The relapse prevention programme is designed for both. Our conclusion was that the mixed groups were more creative and the clients learned from each other's experience. Some groups contained clients who were temporarily on alcohol-sensitising drugs such as Abstem and Antabuse. The above also applied.

Purpose of the interviews

(1) To introduce ourselves to the clients and they to us. This helps to lower the anxiety levels for clients and therapists. Many of the

clients were anxious about groups, and each of their anxieties were addressed by the therapists. The interview also helped lower the therapists' anxiety, in obtaining a 'feel' in advance for the group and group dynamics.

(2) To reduce the dropout rate. Dropout rates can affect the confidence of the therapist and the moods of the remaining group members. Those who in the past did drop out at the first groups had not attended the assessment interview. We felt if the clients got to the interview stage their commitment was pretty strong.

(3) To explain the basic structure of future groups and give a list of topics dealt with in each group.

(4) To demystify groups for many of our clients. The relapse prevention group was often the first group they had ever attended and we wanted it to be a good reference experience for all clients and therapists.

(5) To discover the 'hidden agenda' of the client and to address that agenda; this was our secret 'bait' to keep our client in treatment. We would constantly refer to the client's 'hidden agenda'. The issue involved may not have been completely resolved, but some steps would have been taken to assist the client along this path. This 'secret matching' was the crowd puller.

(6) Exclude those clients who are not suitable for the group.

(7) Encourage regular attendance and commitment.

(8) To identify cognitive errors in the client's thinking.

The interview

We were very fortunate that most of the referrals to the group came from workers on our own team who would speak to us in advance about the referral. It also meant that the client was already familiar with the geography of the building and had probably already been for several interviews with the key worker prior to seeing us. When introduced to the concept of attending group work the client had some image or picture of where this would take place. You will be seeing clients in a variety of locations and you may not have any prior knowledge of a client's history. It may then be necessary to take a history and profile of the client separately from the assessment interview; we assume therapists will know whether or not to take a detailed history. (For more information on a very detailed assessment and history taking, see the introductory chapter.) You may not need a detailed past history – we did not require one when we ran relapse prevention groups for addictive high risk sexual behaviour clients.

Attention to detail
This is a list of points that we have found made a difference:

- All our assessment interviews took place in our group room. The psychogeography remains the same as if a group had just taken place. This helps lower the anxiety for the clients who may never have attended a group before and gets them familiar with the surroundings.

- Prior to the interview all our clients were offered a cup of tea or coffee, as is the normal procedure for any client attending our unit. This we consider a welcoming gesture showing warmth, friendliness and regard for the client. This would allow the client in the waiting area (reception) to relax for a few minutes. However, we did emphasise punctuality so were never late for our interviews.

- Before the interview we had already reviewed any clinical notes available and the referral letter or referral conversation. Our purpose was not to conduct a case history type interview with the client. We paid particular note to how the referring worker thought the client would best benefit from the relapse prevention model. Since there were two of us interviewing, we decided in advance who would ask what questions and concentrate on what issues. While the interviewer paced and led the interviewee, the other noted answers and responses. We had a check-list of interview topics to be covered (see the end of chapter).

- The interviews were approximately half an hour in length. usually we interviewed six clients in each session, i.e. 9.00 AM–12.00 noon, making sure that there was time for feedback and review between each client.

Interview structure

The tour
We started the interview with a tour of the group room, explaining where people sat, where the video camera was located (the room was already laid out as if a group had just finished). Next we showed the client where the toilets were located and finally where the kitchen was. We then sat in the group chairs as the client would in a group and got down to business.

Clearing the cobwebs

We started with finding out what each client already knew about the relapse prevention group – they will have information from the person who referred them and other clients who have already attended. We were interested in their presuppositions. We clarified their previous group experience (if any) and assessed their anxiety about attending. Some clients are worried about self-disclosure, or confronting, or whether the group is like an Alcoholics Anonymous meeting, or other anonymous self-help groups.

We are interested in the belief system of the client (Annis and Davis, 1988). Did they want us to take control and solve their addictive problem? Could they accept the value of learning to prevent relapse? Our aim is that, at the end of the course, they will be their own therapist or maintenance agent.

Can they hack it?

We explained in great detail the time, structure and agenda of each group session. We examined the practical aspects of attending the groups. If clients were working, could they get time off as many of the groups are held during the day. Had they problems getting up early. Did clients have support at home to help them get up and remind them of the group? We spoke briefly to those 'supporters' (partners, relatives) before and after the interview, as they waited for the clients. We explored transport to the groups and asked clients to assess the time involved in travelling. Would they use public or private transport? How was the route organised? We also questioned the client's routine the evening before the group, reminding a client on a controlled drinking programme that during the evening it would be a good idea to abstain. This type of interviewing often brought up some unexpected problems about attending that had not been thought of beforehand and that would have resulted in dropping out. For example, (a) forgetting to mention that a holiday was booked in the middle of the group programme; (b) starting a new job and being unable to take time off; (c) having to look after children.

Housekeeping and homework tasks

An idea borrowed from Alcoholics Anonymous was that each client would be assigned a 'job' for the duration of the group.

- Opening the room.
- Letting clients in.
- Getting the tea/coffee organised.
- Arranging the chairs.

- Emptying the ashtrays (the exception being the groups we ran for smokers).
- Keeping minutes.

Homework tasks were explained after each group and handouts were given to read to prepare for the next group. Also simple tasks were requested, such as keeping a craving diary for one week.

We recorded most of our groups on video and for this we asked our clients' consent (they signed agreement forms). The video would be used in feedback to us the therapists, as well as part of a role-playing session for the clients. We sounded the clients out on how they felt about its use.

Secret matching

Throughout the interview we constantly asked ourselves what is the client's overt or covert agenda for attending the relapse prevention group. (In designing the group to communicate key concepts of the relapse prevention model, we were also connecting these key concepts to the client's personal agenda so that each relapse prevention group was tailor made for each group of clients attending.) Giving clients housekeeping tasks was another way to keep a client in treatment.

Interview conclusion

We concluded the interview by asking the clients to feedback to us what they had learnt, what questions they had. We also gave them a sheet with a review of each session and a reminder of the times, location, etc. (see end of chapter).

Interview post mortem

After the client had left and before the next interview, we reviewed and rated the session.

- Had we sold the relapse prevention model to the client (Scale 0–10)? (That is, is the message getting through?)
- Were they committed to coming (scale 0–10)? (That is, how well is the client receiving the message?)
- Why might they drop out?
- What was their agenda?
- See also the thirteen-point checklist of interview topics, below.

In terms of communication, we rated our and their listening skills. We asked ourselves what we could do differently in the next interview.

Comments on assessment procedure

- We ran the assessment interviews in a relaxed fashion and tried to avoid overwhelming clients with information. We made sure any 'jargon' we used was understood.
- Our belief system was important: that change could be maintained through learning. This fitted in with the 'salesman' style of having a valuable product, the relapse prevention model, to sell.
- Knowing the clients before the interview (if we were the key-workers) helped the process of their attending.

If a client made-it to the assessment interview he or she passed the first hurdle. By changes made in the assessment interview we have been able to reduce the dropout rate considerably (Keaney *et al.*, 1990,

---

Client's name: Date:

THIRTEEN POINT CHECKLIST OF INTERVIEW TOPICS

(1) Interview held in group room.
(2) Assess anxiety levels and previous group experience.
(3) Explain in detail time/structure/agenda of groups.
(4) Explore clients' routine the evening before and the morning of the group.
(5) Any 'supporters' to assist client to the group?
(6) Find task (housekeeping) for duration of group.
(7) Explain 'homework' tasks.
(8) Explain the reason for the video camera and 'sound out' about obtaining permission.
(9) Note 'client agenda' (secret matching).
(10) Ask clients at the end of the interview to feed back what they have learnt.
(11) Rate the interview (scale 1–10):

    (A) Have we sold the model (1–10)?
    (B) Are they committed to coming (1–10)?
    (C) Why might they drop out?

(12) Rate listening skills (scale 1–10):

    (A) Therapists (1–10).
    (B) Client (1–10).

(13) What to do differently next time?

Fig. 2.4.   Checklist of interview topics.

INFORMATION ON THE RELAPSE PREVENTION GROUP

The relapse prevention group is a short course of six two-hour sessions, with plenty of breaks for refreshments. The goal is to deal with the changes you have started and want to continue and also to deal with the hitches; the ups and downs of everyday living, concentrating on practical skills. In moving forward with new attitudes and behaviours, you will have the support of the other group members and course leaders.

Location Ground floor group room

Dates   Tuesdays

(1) 30 January 1990. Getting started. Introductions. A discussion on the positive and negative effects of drinking, both short and long term. An introduction to relaxation.

(2) 6 February 1990. Anxiety. What is it? How to recognise it. How to cope with it.

(3) 13 February 1990. High-risk situations. Review a list of High-risk situations. How to anticipate them. New strategies for dealing with them.

(4) 20 February 1990. Lifestyle balance. What is lifestyle? Looking at stress, changes in routine. Review of 'positive' addictions.

(5) 27 February 1990. Problem solving/thinking errors. How we make decisions. How we fall into thought traps. What the way out is.

(6) 27 March 1990. Depression and review of relapse prevention with emphasis on the coping strategies acquired.

Times   Please arrive at 9.00 AM for 9.15 AM. Coffee/tea is available at 9.00 AM. The group finishes at 11.15 AM. You are most welcome to arrive earlier and to use the room till 12.00 noon, to chat and settle in and to relax before you leave.

We look forward to seeing you at the above times.

Signed by group therapists.

Fig. 2.5. Review of sessions and reminder of the times, dates and location.

in preparation). We considered this interview to set the template for successful groups.

In conclusion, we conducted a detailed and carefully planned assessment procedure in order to develop an individualised programme tailor-made for the needs of our particular client group:

(1) Checklist of interview topics – see Fig. 2.4.
(2) Review of sessions and a reminder of the times/dates and location etc. – see Fig. 2.5.

The first group

A detailed timetable for session 1 is shown in Fig. 2.6.

Pregroup planning session

We first decided on a structure for the group and subsequent groups. Our basic structure was as follows:

(1) Introduce therapists and clients. An introductory talk. Ground rules explained.
(2) Introduce topic of this group – the positive and negative effects of drinking in both short and long term – and the decision balance sheet matrix.
(3) Coffee break.
(4) Continue session topic.
(5) Conclude session topic. Give out homework tasks.
(6) Relaxation exercise.
(7) Complete (A) weekly rating scale, (B) feedback questionnaire.

Comments on the above
Once the first group was over, the subsequent groups were structured as follows:

(1) Open forum (short feedback on where clients were and homework feedback, plus minutes of last group).
(2) Topic for that session.
(3) Coffee break.
(4) Coping with the topic of session.
(5) Homework task.
(6) Relaxation exercises.
(7) Complete form filling.

SESSION TIMETABLE

Aims of the session
- To introduce the group to each other.
- To briefly introduce the relapse prevention model.
- To set the ground rules.
- To discuss the positive and negative effects of drinking, both short term and long term, and the decision balance sheet matrix.
- To distribute homework tasks.
- To learn a relaxation technique.

Time	Title/objective	Content/activity
9.15	Introductions Name game	We introduced ourselves and clients (first names). We asked each client to tell us why they attended (what they wanted to get out of it) and to introduce themselves (first name). (See notes and groundrules.)
9.25	Introductory talk	Reason for the group topics to be covered. Brainstorm on flipchart (see the extract from a typical group at the end of this chapter).
	Ground rules	See notes and ground rules.
	Explanation and aims	
9.45	Initiated discussion on positive and negative effects of drinking both long and short term and of another activity, e.g. sport. Discuss the decision balance sheet matrix.	
10.15	Coffee break	
10.30	Group discussion	Clients were asked what they had learnt from the brainstorm and how they could apply it over the next week.
	Homework tasks	Such as reading anxiety booklet in preparation for the next group.
11.00	Relaxation exercise	See notes and ground rules.
11.15	Form filling	See (1) weekly rating scale and (2) feedback questionnaire (see notes and ground rules).

Fig. 2.6. Detailed timetable for session 1.

Notes and ground rules

Name game
We asked each client to tell us their first name then went around the group in turn, asking each client to repeat their own first name and that of everyone else present. This circuit continued until most of the group could recall each client's name.

Punctuality
We placed a large emphasis on a punctual start and finish. If a client could not attend we asked them to phone us in advance. We asked for a commitment to continue attending the groups.

Smoking
No smoking was allowed except at breaktimes.

Consent for video camera
We asked clients to give us permission to use a video camera. The material would be used by us in the post group therapists' discussion session. Any client not keen on the use of the camera could always sit out of camera range. Clients signed a consent form, as in the example shown in Fig. 2.7.

> I, John ------ consent to the relapse prevention groups being videotaped. I understand that the material will only be used as feedback to the therapists and within the group.

Fig. 2.7. Example consent form for use of video camera.

Housekeeping tasks
We asked for volunteers for the various jobs already mentioned in the assessment interview section, such as tea making.

Confidentiality
We made it clear that what went on in the group stayed in the group.

Stoned or intoxicated behaviour
Clients were asked not to attend if intoxicated/stoned. This was a rule that had only to be enforced once in a three-year period.

Relaxation exercise
We used a variety of relaxation exercises; see Jacobson's relaxation method described in the anxiety booklet.

The following is another short relaxation exercise based on a trance induction by Betty Erickson.

(1) Soft focus your eyes on three objects. Then close eyes.
(2) Listen for three different sounds (e.g. traffic noise).
(3) Notice three different feelings.
(4) Now open eyes and soft focus on two objects, then close eyes.
(5) Listen for two different sounds.
(6) Notice two different feelings (e.g. your breathing).
(7) Open eyes and soft focus on one object, then close eyes.
(8) Listen for one sound.
(9) Notice one feeling.
(10) Sit still for a short period of time.

Homework tasks
We considered homework tasks vital. Examples:

(1) Fill in craving diary.
(2) Note high-risk situations.
(3) Read anxiety booklet.

We strongly urged clients to do them and repeatedly asked for feedback on their homework tasks. This we used in each group which fitted in with the topic of the previous week or preparation for next week.

Form filling
After each group we gave the following forms to fill in. (If detailed evaluation of the model and groups are being done, then other forms/ questionnaires are required. For information on these see Appendix A at the end of the manual and also the introductory chapter.)

Weekly rating scale
This is an anonymous rating scale (0–10, where 0 = most negative and 10 = most positive), measuring six different aspects of the session.

(1) Ability to understand.
(2) Usefulness.
(3) Ability to participate.
(4) Enjoyment.
(5) Atmosphere.
(6) Confidence to deal with problem (e.g. alcohol problem).

Feedback questionnaire
(1) Which part of this session did you find most helpful?

Generally the group discussions about practical solutions were found to be most useful, when all clients had a chance to contribute and share their own experiences.

(2) Which part did you find most difficult?

Most clients mentioned difficulties with identifying their *own* personal weaknesses and problems.

(3) What changes would you like to see?

Several suggestions were made, including more time for relaxation, use of other forms of relaxation and less formality.

(4) Would you like to do any further work?

Some clients mentioned the need for more discussions on what to do about strong cravings and how to facilitate lifestyle changes. A few people pointed out that it would be useful to continue with the groups and/or to meet again occasionally as a group (see section on follow-up session, below).

An extract from a typical group

The aim of this session was to get across to clients the concept that it is possible to replace drinking with other activities which have positive short-term effects and don't have the negative long-term effects of drinking (this will be added to later in the lifestyle intervention group).

Using a flipchart we discussed the good (positive) and bad (negative) effects of drinking in both the short and long term. We did this in the form of a decision making balance sheet matrix. We repeatedly used the idea of a balance sheet across the groups. Often this is at a choice point: do I drink or not? Clients in turn offered suggestions. The following list shows the result of their discussions.

Positives	Negatives
Short term	*Short term*
Relaxing	Poor memory
Sociable (increase)	Poor concentration
Confidence (increase)	Blackouts
Easier to express yourself	Hangovers
High	Shakes
Occupies time	Fearful
Lessens anxiety	'Letting yourself go'
Creates an atmosphere	Regrets
Nice taste	Guilt/disappointment
Nice feeling expectation	Anxiety
	'Odd one out'
	Loss of responsibility
Long term	*Long term*
Memory loss	Lowers career prospects
Helps forget unwanted thoughts	Impairs judgement
Blocks out	Burden
Emotional anaesthetic	Negative role model
Aids sleep	Depression
Being part of a group	Increases anxiety
Delaying making a decision	Trouble with law
Release	Addiction
	Drink driving
	Increases accidents at home/work
	Suicide
	Health problems
	Antisocial behaviour
	Change in appearance
	Memory loss
	Loss of contact with friends
	Isolated
	Vulnerable
	Loss of jobs/days at work
	Violence

Then we looked at sport in the same way. The clients and therapists continued brainstorming.

Positives	Negatives
Short term	*Short term*
Sociable	Tiredness and lethargy
Feel good	Overdoing it
Fitness	Obligation to drink afterwards
Aids sleeping	More/less alcohol intake
Tires you out	Loss of self-esteem
Occupies time	
Relaxed/unwind	
Meeting people	
Release	
Fresh air	
Long term	*Long term*
Regular exercise	Injury
Reduces stress	Too much commitment
Healthy	Fanatical/addictive
Interest	Expense
Travel	Heart attacks for joggers
Self-discipline	
Responsibility	
Positive attitude	
Achievement	

The group noted that short-term effects for both are quite similar. Many of the short-term effects for sport carry through to the long term and remain positive while few of the short-term effects of drinking carry through and the subsequent effects tend to be negative. The similarities between the lists show that drinking can be replaced with other activities to fill your time. This we shall be looking at again in a later group (see Chapter 9).

Dropouts

When clients dropped out of the group unannounced we did as follows:

(1) Wrote to them inviting them to the next week's groups (sometimes because they had a 'slip' clients felt they would not be welcomed back).
(2) Where possible also phoned them, inviting them to return.
(3) We offered individual appointments.
(4) Usually we have a good attendance for the first two groups. One of the reasons we assume people drop out is that the 'material' or topic starts to hit close to home (for example dealing with cognitive error denial) and the client can't handle it.

Finishing the group

Group dynamics are such that the last two groups were very fruitful. Many clients expressed a wish that the programme could continue. We made it clear from the start that the programme had a certain lifespan but could act as a conduit to progress into other types of groups or individual work. We referred clients to:

- Individual psychotherapy.
- In-patient treatment programmes.
- Drinkwatchers.
- Support groups.
- Self-help groups.

Follow-up session

This session took place one month after the final group meeting. The aims of the session included:

- Finding out about the progress of the clients in relation to their treatment goals.
- Identifying the changes clients incorporated into their lives following attendance at the relapse prevention groups.
- Sharing with other clients personal benefits and difficulties in coping with abstinence/controlled drinking.
- To function as a top-up or refresher session.
- To enable data collecting for evaluation of the programme.
- Identifying any needs concerning further support and highlighting other treatment choices at our unit.

References

Annis, H.M. and Davis, C.S. (1988) 'Relapse Prevention'. In R.K. Hester and W.R. Miller (Eds) *Handbook of Alcoholism Treatment Approaches*. Pergamon Press, Inc., New York.

Donovan, D.M. and Marlatt, G.A. (Eds) (1988) *Assessment of Addictive Behaviors*. Guilford Press, New York.

Gossop, M. (Ed) (1989) *Relapse and Addictive Behaviour*. Tavistock/Routledge, London.

Marlatt, G.A. and Gordon, J.R. (1985). *Relapse Prevention: Maintenance Strategies in the Treatment of Addictive Behaviors*. Guilford Press, New York.

Chapter 3

Anxiety

Anxiety is something that everyone experiences from time to time. It is a normal reaction that occurs in ordinary people in response to externally (environmentally) and internally (cognitively) produced stimuli.

Anxiety is a complex reaction which was crucial to our survival in the past when man lived in more natural conditions. It is our 'fight or flight' reaction to danger or an emergency. This involves channelling our energy or charging up our bodies and minds to deal with the threat.

Unfortunately this reaction is of very little use for many situations we encounter in our modern way of life. Many of the threats are psychological and we can not physically fight our way out of them or run away. Also subtle psychological triggers may turn on the system in wholly inappropriate situations (in supermarkets, when travelling in a tube train). This phenomenon is more commonly known as a 'panic attack'.

For some people a specific situation or object becomes the trigger for the anxiety reaction. This is commonly described as having a 'phobia' for a situation or object. Examples of this would be fear of social situations – social phobia; fear of spiders – arachnaphobia.

At times anxiety can be useful. It can be turned into an advantageous experience and need not be seen as a negative reaction. Everyone can benefit by learning to control their level of anxiety.

Anxiety can cover a broad range of experiences and can mean different things to different people. A person may experience different symptoms of anxiety at different times.

If you ask a group of people what happens to them when they feel anxious they could give any of the following replies:

Palpitations	'Butterflies'
Cold and clammy	Being overwhelmed
Fear	Hot flushes
Nausea	Panic
Catastrophic thoughts	Tense
Sweaty	Restless
Confusion	

Rachman (1978) has proposed a model that makes it easier to understand the anxiety response. Rachman described three components of anxiety:

(1) Physiological – the bodily reactions.
(2) Cognitive – the thinking reactions.
(3) Behaviourial – the person's actions.

When an individual experiences anxiety all three components come into play. The person, however, may only be aware of one or two elements, such as sweaty palms and hot flushes (physiological). An observer may be aware of the individual's restlessness (behavioural). From our own experience we have found that clients are least aware of the cognitive/thinking component. Each client needs to be helped into an increased awareness of all the possible components of anxiety and, more importantly, to learn and practise the appropriate coping mechanisms.

The link between anxiety and addictive behaviours

Many people take some form of action to cope with anxiety. They may avoid a particular situation, or develop a strategy or specific course of action to deal with the anxiety. People with an addiction problem often use their addictive behaviour as their way or strategy for coping with anxiety. The addictive behaviour brings them short-term and immediate relief (the 'quick fix') from the discomfort or distress they may experience (a pull on a cigarette).

Individuals who are anxious, timid or who feel socially inadequate are more likely to experience an alleviation of such feelings after indulging in their addiction of choice (Glatt, 1982). The relief from feelings of anxiety is inherently rewarding, so that the behaviour is more likely to be repeated. A tense, anxious individual may hit the 'quick fix' and, after finding such response works, may then not learn more adaptive ways of coping. When next feeling anxious the individual is more likely to use what they experience works for them fast – for example, reaching for the tranquillisers. The rapid relief is what is recalled rather than the longer-term unwanted effects.

The second link between anxiety and addiction is the compounding effect of withdrawal symptoms with anxiety. The physiological withdrawal symptoms from some substances, such as minor tranquillisers, are anxiety producing. Added to this is the anxiety caused by worries and concerns about controlling the addiction. The heightened level of anxiety that a client is likely to experience because of these factors is likely to enhance the probability of a relapse and create a vicious cycle.

The vicious cycle of anxiety, withdrawal effects and use of chemicals is one that many clients find themselves in and are unable to climb out of. The therapist needs to communicate to the client that there are different ways of dealing or coping with their anxiety and ways of breaking the cycle that they find themselves in.

Coping with anxiety

Most people cope with anxiety most of the time. Those of us who have difficulties with anxiety can successfully learn techniques to cope. One method of effectively teaching coping skills for anxiety is stress inoculation training (Meichenbaum and Jaremko 1983). We have used this approach successfully in our relapse prevention programme.

The approach involves three phases (Cameron and Meichenbaum 1982):

(1) The client understands the concepts and is then able to make an informed judgement regarding the situation.
(2) Learning of new appropriate coping skills or relearning old coping skills.
(3) Rehearsal and application of the newly acquired skills.

A vital part of the relapse prevention model is the imparting of information. Explanation of the thinking (cognitive), actions (behavioural) and bodily (physiological) mechanisms in operation when a person is feeling anxious is of crucial importance. Time spent on helping the client grasp the concepts of anxiety is invaluable.

It may also correct any misconceptions that the client may have concerning the nature of anxiety – perhaps the idea that feeling out of control when anxious indicates that they are going mad. Challenging their negative internal dialogue (automatic thoughts) is a major factor in this process. A clearer overview allows the client to make a more informed decision about his or her problem and how to tackle it.

To the therapist it may appear that you are often stating the obvious. Offering clients a way of understanding their anxiety will increase their sense of control and therefore increase self-confidence (self-efficacy).

Relaxation techniques can be used as a general strategy for coping with anxiety. In addition individuals may need to develop specific strategies, such as positive thinking, to cope with anxiety provoking situations. A typical session timetable is given in Fig. 3.1.

SESSION TIMETABLE
ANSIETY AND RELAXATION

Aim of the session

- To increase the group's awareness of anxiety and appropriate ways to cope with anxiety.

Time (minutes)	Objective	Content/activity
5	Discover what group members understand by 'anxiety'	Each number of the group to say one sentence about their understanding of anxiety.
		Pick out key words on flipchart.
10	Identify different components of anxiety	Therapist to outline components:
		Cognitive factors – thought processes, unique to each person, loss of control of mind, depersonalisation, detachment, negative thinking 'errors' in thinking and perception.
10		Physical factors – 'fight or flight', palpitations, dizziness, hot flushes, nausea, diarrhoea, muscle tension, headaches, sweating.
10		Behaviourial factors – avoidance ('flight'), taking alcohol or drugs, fighting.
		Using each of these factors to brainstorm for the group's personal experiences of anxiety.

10	List different ways of coping with each component of anxiety	Therapist talk: Cognitive – identifying negative thoughts, identifying thinking errors, positive thinking, correcting the above, self-talk.
10	Be able to demonstrate positive thinking	Ask each member to give a positive thinking statement about themselves and record it.
10	To increase self-awareness of how others perceive each member	Ask each member to give a positive thinking statement about the member to their left or right and record it.
	Be able to identify appropriate occasions to utilise positive statements	Cards with statements to be carried and used by clients when negative thoughts occur. Identify personal anxiety situations to use cards.
10		Therapist talk: Physical – meditation, controlled breathing, relaxation.
20	Participate in a relaxation exercise	Therapist to lead Jacobson's relaxation method.
	Experience the ability to feel relaxed through active exercise	

Session to include

15 mins 'Open frame' to allow for feedback
10 mins Coffee break

Fig. 3.1. Session timetable: anxiety and relaxation.

Notes for therapists

The following section on thought processes is structured to help therapists teach coping techniques in terms of the three-component model. It is written in a style that should enable it to be used directly in handouts. See also Chapter 5.

Thought processes

Identifying negative thinking and thinking errors

- Research shows that feelings of anxiety (bodily reactions) are often preceded by thoughts associated with it. These thoughts are sometimes difficult to identify because they are 'automatic' and flash through your mind quickly. These thoughts can be identified if you look out for them.
- When beginning to feel anxious 'stop' for a moment to examine what is 'going through your mind'.
- Write down your 'thoughts' when feeling anxious.
- Keep a diary (daily record) of your thoughts and feelings.

You will invariably find on closer inspection that these thoughts are of a 'negative nature', generally unpleasant and are full of 'errors'.

Errors in thinking include exaggerations (tendency to view things in an extreme way), false assumptions, irrational and illogical thinking and tendencies to ignore positive experiences.

With this 'insight' we can now set about the task of modifying our thinking. Here are a few simple techniques that have been helpful to many people in 'coping with' and overcoming anxiety and other negative emotions.

Positive thinking

Try to substitute each recognised negative thought with a positive thought. One way of doing this is called the 'two column technique'.

Divide a card or piece of paper into two columns. Write down your identified negative thoughts in the left-hand column and for each negative thought write down one or two positive alternatives in the right-hand column, see Fig. 3.2.

Carry this card or piece of paper with you and use it in situations of anxiety, both to jot down negative thoughts and to remind you of

NEGATIVE	POSITIVE
I can never go to a supermarket with all those people without embarrassing myself.	I am going to try to go to the supermarket and when I do it will be a real achievement.
	I have been able to go to a supermarket before, so I can go again.

Fig. 3.2.

positive alternatives. Keep repeating the positive alternatives to yourself (self-talk).

Correcting thinking errors

Questioning assumptions
A lot of our thinking errors are based on long-established false assumptions that we have taken for granted. The formula here is to look at and identify assumptions related to your anxiety and to make a list of them.

For each assumption write down the answers to the following questions:

(1) Why do I think this way?
(2) How true is it?
(3) What would happen if I thought differently or acted differently.

Once you become aware of your assumptions and question them you may find that this in itself will lead to a change in your thinking. You will find it useful to discuss them with a friend or a counsellor.

After identifying them you may need to test out some deep-rooted assumptions to convince yourself that they were wrong. Setting up experiments/situations to test out assumptions is a very useful exercise and should prove very helpful toward changing thinking.

- *Assumption.* Most people have no difficulty in talking to strangers.
- *Experiment.*

(1) Observe people when they are talking to strangers.
(2) Ask people you know about how they feel when talking to strangers.

- *Results.* Does it confirm or refute your assumption? If it refutes your assumption write down your modified assumption. For example: 'Most people have some difficulty in talking to strangers.'

Checking exaggerations

The formula described above for questioning assumptions can be used to correct and deal with other 'thinking errors' such as exaggerations.

Once again look at your thinking associated with anxiety. Try to pick out the thoughts you think could possibly represent a 'blown up' or 'magnified' view of a negative experience. For example:

> 'I had a panic attack on the tube, I will never be able to go on the tube again. I always have panic attacks on tubes.'

Do you really? Can you remember any instances when you didn't? If you can, then you have exaggerated the problem!

Once you have identified the exaggerated negative thoughts, question them; if appropriate test them out, talk to people about them, think of positive alternatives and get them into perspective.

Bodily reactions

The body reacts in a 'fight or flight' manner. Our systems charge up as a result of the secretion of adrenalin into our blood stream. We are now going to deal with methods of 'turning off' the system.

Progressive relaxation training

This is a method of learning to induce a state of physical 'relaxation' by tensing and relaxing groups of muscles in a systematic way. The rationale of this is to teach people the 'skill' of 'relaxing'. Like any skill (cycling, swimming, etc.), you need to practice regularly to master it. It is expected that this would lead to the development of a 'feel' or a 'mental picture' of a 'state of being relaxed'. This could then be used to induce a state of relaxation or counteract anxiety in an 'anxiety situation' without going through the whole tensing and relaxing muscle process.

Relaxation exercise 1

The script below could be used to start your progressive relaxation training. It should be practised two or three times a day. Once the skill feels as if it has been mastered, proceed to gradually reduce the groups of muscles used until the state of relaxation can be induced by mental means with minimal muscle exercise.

'Before beginning this relaxation exercise find a comfortable chair to sit in. Loosen any tight clothing, remove spectacles if you wear them and ensure that you are warm enough. You are now ready to begin.

'Close your eyes and concentrate on your breathing. Take a deep breath in, hold it, and breath out. Then repeat. Take a deep breath in, hold it, and breath out. Keep your breathing rhythm steady. During the relaxation exercise I will be asking you to tense and relax various muscles; you will find it easier to inhale when tensing and exhale when relaxing.

'Screw up your eyes as tightly as possible, clench your teeth and purse your lips. Feel the muscles in your face tighten and then feel the tension fall away as you allow the muscles to relax. And again as you breathe in screw up your eyes tightly, clench your teeth and purse your lips, and slowly breathe out as you allow your muscles to relax. Once more tighten the muscles in your face and hold before slowly breathing out and letting the muscles relax.

'Keep breathing in a steady rhythm and raise your shoulders to your ears. Allow your shoulders to fall as you breathe out. Repeat this twice more, feeling the tension in your neck and shoulders fall away.

'Now tighten your muscles in your upper arms like a strong man and hold for a while before relaxing and breathing out. Tense the muscles in the upper arms and feel how heavy they are when you relax them.

'Now clench your hands to make a fist, hold them for a while and then relax. Again, make your hands into a fist, hold and gently allow your fingers to uncurl.

'Take a deeper breath in and feel the muscles in your chest and stomach being expanded. Hold and slowly breathe out. Repeat this deeper breath in, hold it and breathe out. Allow your breathing to return to its gentle rhythmic pattern.

'Now tighten the muscles of your stomach, and gradually breathe out as you relax them. Again pull in your stomach muscles, hold and relax. Once more, tense your stomach muscles, hold and relax as you breath out.

'Now work the muscles on your lower back and buttocks. Tighten them, hold and relax. And repeat this a further two times.

'As you take your next breath in tighten the muscles in your upper legs. Keep the tension for a while and then relax as you exhale. Tense this set of muscles twice more.

'Now point your toes up towards your body and tense the muscles in your calves. Hold and then allow your muscles to relax. Repeat this once more. Your legs and feet should now feel heavy.

'Continue to breathe evenly. Your body now feels relaxed and comfortable, and is sinking into the chair with heaviness. Allow your mind to drift with pleasant thoughts.

'When you wish to end the relaxation exercises slowly open your eyes and gradually move your body, becoming aware of your surroundings. You will now be feeling calm, refreshed, relaxed and awake.'

Relaxation exercise 2
Here is another method that can be used to reduce anxiety and induce a state of relaxation.

'Close your eyes and start by taking a deep breath in, hold it and gently breathe out. And again breathe in, hold, and slowly breathe out. Keep your breathing steady throughout this exercise.

'Imagine that your body is full of fine, soft sand, and that you have small holes in your fingertips and toes.

'The sand gradually leaves your body through your toes and fingers. Feel the sand filter out of your body and as it does so feel your body become limp and heavy.

'Allow your head to drop forward as the sand starts to leave your body. As the level drops your arms and abdomen feel heavy and limp and sink into the back of the chair.

'You can feel the sand draining slowly from your legs and as it does the muscles in your legs feel relaxed and limp.

'As the final grains of sand fall from your toes your whole body feels relaxed, comfortable and heavy. Keep your eyes closed and your breathing slow and steady and allow your mind to drift away with pleasant and peaceful thoughts.

'When you wish to end the relaxation exercise gradually open your eyes and become aware of your surroundings. Gradually move your arms and legs. You will now be feeling calm, refreshed, relaxed and awake.'

Meditation

People in the East, in countries such as India or China have been practising anxiety management for thousands of years. In fact this is true of many ancient civilisations. One method that is deeply engrained in Asian religions and culture is meditation. Meditation is considered by them to be crucial for a person's 'well-being'. Unfortunately it is only recently that the benefits of meditation have been realised in the West.

There are hundreds of methods and techniques of meditation. Described below is one simple technique that could be used as an introduction. For those who want to find out more about meditation there are numerous books available on the subject (see Appendix B).

Meditative exercise

First of all find a quiet and comfortable place where you won't be disturbed.

You can either sit on the floor, on a mat or cushion, or on a chair where you can keep your back straight. Adopt a position that is comfortable (if you are sitting on the floor you could cross your legs, but do not attempt the lotus position if you are not used to it, as it could be harmful).

Close your eyes and imagine you are in a dark room. Take a deep breath slowly through your nose (counting up to ten, or as near as you can). Hold your breath for the same number of counts as it took you to breath in. Now slowly exhale through your mouth taking the same number of counts. Once you have emptied your lungs, prevent yourself from breathing in for an equal number of counts as before. Repeat the process from the beginning.

Try to practice this meditation for five minutes, two or three times a day.

You should try to concentrate only on your breathing and you can use mental images to help you do this. One useful image would be to imagine the breathing process as a flow of water or light running along the sides of a square.

Once the breathing process becomes automatic (not having to think about it) you can start to direct your mind to other things. At this stage attempt the process of trying to 'empty' your mind by throwing out all impinging thoughts.

Breathing and blanking out your mind, practised with discipline, should result in your developing the ability to induce a deep state of relaxation when needed, and a general sense of 'well-being'.

Coping with panic

One person in three experiences panic attacks. Often extra help is needed to cope with these. The fear of panic attacks can be sufficient to trigger one off. In order to cope with a panic attack it is important to remember that the feelings are nothing more than an exaggeration of normal bodily reactions to stress.

The feelings are not harmful or dangerous – just unpleasant. Nothing worse will happen. In a panic people have catastrophic thoughts, such as 'I will die of a heart attack'. Most people's catastrophe thoughts are the same each time, so replace these with positive self statements designed to counter them.

Learning to cope with panic attacks is a matter of practice. Each attack is an opportunity to practise and learn something new. Anxiety follows a natural pattern; it rises, reaches a plateau, and then slowly subsides. Simply by waiting the fear will begin to slowly fade away. It is important to stay in the situation and not run away.

While staying with the feelings:

(1) Use a brief relaxation exercise.
(2) Repeat the positive self-statements.
(3) Think about the progress you have made despite all the difficulties, and how pleased you will be when you succeed this time.
(4) Look around you and focus on the details of the surroundings.
(5) When you are ready to leave, start off in an easy relaxed way.

Put the instructions on a cue card that is easy to carry around.

References

Cameron, R. and Meichenbaum, D. (1982) 'The Nature of Effective Coping and the Treatment of Stress Related Problems: A Cognitive-Behaviourial Perspective.' In L. Goldberger and S. Breznitz (Eds.) *Handbook of Stress*. Free Press, London.

Glatt, M. (1982) *Alcoholism*. Hodder and Stoughton, Kent.

Meichenbaum, D. and Jaremko, M. (1983) *Stress Reduction and Prevention*. Plenum, New York.

Rachman, S. (1978) 'Human Fears: A Three-system Analysis', *Scandinavian Journal of Behaviour Therapy*, **7**, 237–45.

Chapter 4

High-Risk Situations

Background on high-risk situations

Why have a group on high-risk situations?

The reason for having a group on high-risk situations is because all the research on relapse prevention confirms that adequate handling of these situations increases dramatically the probability of maintaining the behavioural change (abstinence or control of the addiction in question), so much so that some therapists are running programmes dealing only with high-risk situations (Annis and Davis, 1988).

In Marlatt and Gordon's model, when a client encounters a high-risk situation it is a testing point.

Outcome A: They have an adequate coping response (a cognitive/behavioural one). This increases their self-confidence to deal with the situation and decreases the probability of a lapse or relapse.

Outcome B: They have an inadequate coping response, their self confidence to deal with the situation is decreased. They believe they cannot control their use of the substance. This increases the probability of a lapse or relapse.

Example
John is a 41-year-old married man who has abstained from alcohol for two weeks after a daily drinking pattern of five years. He attends an extended family Sunday lunch. His relatives are unaware of this change and pressurise him to drink.

- *Outcome A*: Attending his weekly relapse prevention group he has anticipated this situation (an input into his thinking) has rehearsed three responses (role-playing with other group members) and feels confident he can dealt with it (positive emotional state).

- *Outcome B*:   He is taken by surprise, confused how to respond and thinks 'I can limit myself to two drinks'.

What is a lapse and what is a relapse?

A *lapse* would be an indulgence in the addictive behaviour over a short period of time: for example, having stopped smoking for three weeks Jane has three cigarettes one evening when feeling fatigued. The following day she is back on her programme of smoking cessation.

A *relapse* is where the old behaviour is recommenced over a longer period of time: for example, Peter has been clean for two months, then meets a dealer by chance and scores daily for the next four days. A relapse is seen as a failure to maintain the change rather than a failure to initiate the change (Annis and Davis, 1988).

Is it so simple that one situation can trigger a relapse?

We found it helpful to think in terms of relapse being a process operating on a number of levels. We acknowledge that several reasons could be responsible for the relapse episode and that these reasons are often interlinked; also that, time after time, clients describe the same situations across a number of contexts and addictions. In terms of responding to the high-risk situations, we can prescribe a number of specific responses as well as more global responses (see Chapter 9 for lifestyle balance).

Defining and identifying high-risk situations

Historical background

Working with clients and their relatives and listening to their descriptions of relapse episodes, we have noted the similarities in their stories. The friends, relatives and clients often spot the change in behaviour, feelings and comments made in the specific situations that lead to a relapse.

Alcoholics Anonymous founded in the 1930s, noted in a 1974 publication the following:

A checklist of symptoms leading to relapse

(1) Exhaustion.
(2) Dishonesty.
(3) Impatience.
(4) Argumentativeness.
(5) Depression.
(6) Frustration.
(7) Self-pity.
(8) Cockiness.
(9) Complacency.
(10) Expecting too much from others.
(11) Letting up on disciplines (prayer, meditation, daily inventory, Alcoholics Anonymous attendance).
(12) Use of mood-altering chemicals.
(13) Wanting too much.
(14) Forgetting gratitude.
(15) 'It can't happen to me.'
(16) Omnipotence (this is a feeling that results from a combination of many of the above – you now have all the answers for yourself and others; no-one can tell you anything).

In recent research on the process of relapse Marlatt and Gordon (1980) analysed 311 initial relapse episodes obtained from clients with a variety of problem behaviours (problem drinking, smoking, heroin addiction, compulsive gambling and overeating). They identified three primary high-risk situations that were associated with almost three quarters of all the relapses reported. (It is not our intention to give a detailed description of this but just to highlight the important findings as they relate to the running of groups – see 'The Big Three', below.)

Definition of a high-risk situation

While remaining clean or abstinent, Marlatt and Gordon's model pre-supposes that a client experiences a sense of perceived control. The behaviour is 'under control' so long as it does not occur during this period. The longer the period of successful abstinence, the greater the client's perception of self-control and the greater confidence the client has in making a positive choice.

However, thinking (cognitive) strategies and patterns of behaviour are strong. Doing things one way for many years takes time to alter. Many of these behaviours are on the borders of consciousness. The client is on 'automatic pilot'. The perceived control will continue until a high-risk situation is encountered.

A high-risk situation is defined broadly as any situation which poses a threat to the client's sense of control and increases the risk of potential relapse. Without the appropriate coping skills, the most common response to a high-risk situation is a lapse or more probably a relapse.

'The big three'

Research (Marlatt and Gordon, 1980) shows three areas associated with high rates of relapse:

(1) 'Downers' (negative emotional states)
(2) 'Rows' (interpersonal conflict)
(3) 'Joining the club' (social pressure).

'Downers'

It is our impression that most lapses/relapses occur because clients want to change the unpleasant way they feel and to make that change fast. We think this is a factor in all relapses (except those caused by positive emotional states).

Negative emotional states are where the client is experiencing a mood or feeling, such as frustration, anger, anxiety, sadness, depression or boredom, prior to or at the same time as the lapse occurs (35% of all relapses in Marlatt and Gordon's 1980 study).

Example
'I had been dry for two weeks and had so much more time on my hands. Besides working I had no other plans since up to this all my free time was spent drinking. Come Saturday night I was *bored* and *angry* that I was making all this effort and getting nowhere fast. Without thinking, I found myself in a bar, one of my usual haunts, and got plastered as fast as I could.'

These feelings within the client (intrapersonal) were perhaps previously dealt with by indulging in the addictive behaviour.

'Rows'

Interpersonal conflicts are situations involving an ongoing or relatively recent conflict associated with any interpersonal (one-to-one) relationship such as marriage, friendship, family members or employer/employee. Arguments and confrontations occur commonly here (16 per cent in Marlatt and Gordon's 1980 study).

Example
'I went to see a social worker who was arranging a move from a hostel to a flat for me. I had to wait about 20 minutes, then I discovered that my application was still being processed after one month. Well I blew my top, told everyone where to get off and got into *an argument* with the head of the social services department. I left feeling helpless that I was at the mercy of the system. The only way to get rid of this headache was to use, so I went out and bought some smack.'

'Joining the club'

According to Marlatt's study, social pressure accounts for 20% of the relapses. These are situations in which the client is responding to the influence of another person or group of people who exert pressure on the client to engage in the taboo behaviour.

Social pressure may be direct (direct interpersonal contact with verbal persuasion) or indirect (being in the presence of others who are engaging in the same target behaviour, even though no direct pressure is involved).

Example
'Colin's dealer had been phoning him. So far Colin had put her off since he started on the methadone programme. However, she was not

content with losing such a valuable customer so she called at his flat and found him in. Colin *felt pressurised* and bought two days' supply of heroin.

Identifying high-risk situations

In anticipating and preparing for high-risk situations, the client needs to be familiar with the ones common to most individuals and also his or her own unique ones. Clients need to know that, no matter how well prepared, they can be caught unaware.

The purpose, then, of running this group is to educate the client to identify and anticipate high-risk situations and learn effective coping responses.

Interviews

We noted that clients, from their first interview through detoxification and after, are giving information about high-risk situations, though often not in the language we use. Without our direct questions we listened and noted the triggers and cues clients described leading up to, immediately prior to and during relapses. So phase one in identifying high-risk situations is to develop an awareness in all our interviews of the language of high-risk situations.

The use of questionnaires/exercises

We have used a number of questionnaires to identify high-risk situations in the following contexts.

- In a one-to-one session.
- Prior to the group on high-risk situations, so clients have some preparation.
- As an evaluation tool to monitor clients' progress to cope with high-risk situations in the above-mentioned contexts.

Examples of questionnaires that can be used for assessing problem drinkers are:

(1) Inventory of Drinking Situations (IDS–100) (Annis, 1982). This is a 100-item self-report questionnaire which provides a profile of situations in which the client drank heavily over the past year. Eight categories of drinking situations are assessed: unpleasant

emotions, physical discomfort, pleasant emotions, testing control over alcohol, urges and temptations to drink, conflict with others, pressure from others to drink, and pleasant times with others. From this assessment a hierarchy of high risk drinking situations for the client is developed.

(2) Situational Confidence Questionnaire (SCQ–39) (Annis, 1984). This provides a measure of the client's current level of confidence in coping with a range of drinking situations. From this assessment a hierarchy of drinking situations is constructed which forms the basis for negotiating with the client on how to cope and reviewing regularly how the client is doing in the programme.

Details of these questionnaires and similar instruments for other addictions can be found in a recent text on assessment of addictive behaviours by Donovan and Marlatt (1988).

The use of drink diaries/craving diaries

Prior to a client setting a goal we asked them to monitor the addictive behaviour (smoking, drinking, etc.). We used their diary, e.g. drink diary, (Fig. 4.1) to provide us with clues of their high-risk situations. (See also Appendix A(I).)

After they had a programme plan we asked them to keep a craving diary (Fig. 4.2).

Comparing the information in both diaries, there is often a correlation of high-risk situations. A lot of this information is not available to the client until an exercise like this is undertaken.

Emotional states exercise

As negative emotional states are involved in most cases of lapse/ relapse, an exercise we developed was to find out what were the range of emotional states our clients experienced on a daily basis.

Emotional state log
This is a 24-hour log kept on working and rest days. The client fills in on an hourly basis the predominant emotional state he or she feels.

Emotional state choices
We presented the client with a list of emotional states (Fig. 4.3). We asked them to circle what states they recognised. We also asked them

Day	Time of drinking	Number of units	Type of alcohol	In company or alone	Location of drinking	Feelings before/after	Effects of drinking	Cost

Fig. 4.1. Drink diary.

Day/Date	Place	Time/who with	Describe how you felt	Action taken

Fig. 4.2. Craving diary.

Anxiety	Amused	Apathy
Hope	Responsible	Curious
Confused	Joy	Motivated
Purposeful	Anger	Concern
Affectionate	Resentful	Ambition
Dread	Frustration	Thrilled
Happy	Patient	Fulfilled
Fear	Satisfied	Embarrassed
Grief	Capable	Resourceful
Anticipation	Disappointment	Bored
Delight	Guilty	Depressed
Excited	Lonely	Cranky
Disagreeable	Ashamed	Resistant
Hurt	Longing	Determined
Regret	Amorous	Apprehensive
Dissatisfied	Inadequate	Challenged
Ethusiasm	Worthwhile	Secure
Sexy	Connected	Playful
Passionate	Grateful	Furious
Trusting	Naughty	Acceptance
Annoyed	Irritated	Content
Envy	Wary	Suspicious
Jealous	Confident	Sad
Creative	Inspired	Awe
Friendly	Assertive	Greedy

Fig. 4.3. Emotional states.

to add to the list, as many clients had their own unique states not in our list.

Prior to the group on high-risk situations, a suggested homework task is as shown in Fig. 4.4.

Risk management: coping with high-risk situations

Definition of coping

Coping is defined as a form of *action* to reduce a danger, correct a harm and/or achieve a planned goal. Coping is a *response* to a given situation such as those described as high-risk situations.

We divide coping into:

---

(1) Please list below five situations that have been or continue to be high-risk situations for you to relapse.

    (1) ....
    (2) ....
    (3) ....
    (4) ....
    (5) ....

(2) Please write a short description of how you have coped or now cope with the above situations.

    (1) ....
    (2) ....
    (3) ....
    (4) ....
    (5) ....

Please bring this questionnaire with you to the group on high-risk situations.

Fig. 4.4. Homework task.

(1) *Specific coping strategies*
- *Skills training.* If skills are absent each client can develop, through practice and concentration, a repertoire or collection of special skills/techniques to help avoid relapse (if skills are absent). If skills are inhibited clients can learn to facilitate disinhibition and reduce anxiety/fear (behavioural rehearsal, instruction, evaluative feedback, modelling and role-playing).
- *Cognitive reframing.* Here we encourage alternative perspectives/cognitions. We stress the 'learning' quality of relapse prevention: 'There is no failure, only feedback.' We use coping imagery, homework tasks and tackle errors of thinking.

(2) *Global coping strategies*
Lifestyle interventions (see Chapter 9) aim to increase the client's coping strategies across contexts, using meditation, relaxation, 'balanced lifestyle', etc.

Specific coping strategies: overview

- General principles.
- Homework assignments.

- Coping with a lapse.
- Coping with panic.
- Coping with anger.
- Coping with craving.
- Coping with depression.
- Use of sensitising drugs in high-risk situations.

General principles in coping with high-risk situations

(1) In risk management our overall principle was to move the client from a resourceless state to a resourceful state.
(2) We explored with the client resources available in the community, for example family and friends who provided support, people at work, agencies (Alcoholics Anonymous, Narcotics Anonymous) and individuals (minister).
(3) We wondered what the client had done before to successfully avoid or leave a high-risk situation (past resources, what worked before).
(4) We asked about the client's thinking process: flexible or rigid?
(5) We knew that the client having a wide range of coping responses increased our success rate.
(6) We emphasised early recognition of warning cues ('forewarned is forearmed').
(7) We determined the adequacy/deficiency of existing coping skills.
(8) We stressed that an awareness of cues should alert the client to implement coping strategies (just as a motorist will respond to traffic signs whilst driving).
(9) We emphasised high-risk situations as 'forks in the road'/points of choice, and opportunities for new learning.

Homework assignments

We used self-monitoring techniques as a source for identifying warning cues. We asked clients to monitor specific situations/cognitions. We were interested in specific details on a daily basis. We wanted to know the immediate antecedents, the associated thoughts and feelings and the attempted coping responses. This was useful in revealing important triggers and planning alternatives.

Anticipating problem situations is an important skill to develop and we thought in terms of a high-risk situation Filofax (see Fig. 4.5). We asked clients to fill this in. We advised them to plan and rehearse mentally their coping responses, to have a number of alternatives,

Side A			Side B		
Day/date	Anticipated HRS	Planned strategy	Actual strategy used	Ratings (1–10)	
				Comment	Control

Complete side (A) prior to the actual day.   Complete side (B) at the end of the day.

Fig. 4.5.   Filofax for planning and coping with high-risk situations.

what they actually used, and how confident and comfortable they felt.

Gradually we wanted the clients to practise new behaviours in increasingly more difficult situations (Annis and Davis, 1988).

Coping with a lapse

(Modified from Marlatt and Gordon, 1980.)

We take the example of drinking. If a lapse occurs:

- Wait 20 minutes.
- Review the positives and negatives of continued drinking.
- Ring an emergency number.

We asked clients to carry with them a reminder card with instructions on what to do if a lapse occurs, a decision balance sheet (kept up to date) regarding a decision for abstinence and the phone number of a sympathetic friend. (We also put the phone number of our relapse prevention helpline on the card – see Chapter 2.)

Generalised ways of coping with a lapse
(1) Have a drink of water, fruit juice, mineral water.
(2) Read, watch television, listen to the radio or to music.
(3) Go out for a walk, get into company.
(4) Have something sweet to eat.
(5) Give yourself a treat.

(6) Have a special non-alcoholic drink for special reasons, e.g. Aqua Libra, Perrier with ice and lemon.

(7) Take a bottle of non-alcoholic drink to a special occasion.

(8) Do not have drink in the house.

A more specific coping strategy

(1) *Stop, look and listen.* When a lapse occurs *stop* what you are doing and think. This is a warning that you are in danger. Think of it as a flat tyre: the driver stops at a safe place to deal with it. Look at your 'reminder card' for instructions.

(2) *Keep calm.* Remember, one slip does not make a total relapse. A slip does not mean you are a failure and have no willpower or that you are a hopeless addict. There is no failure, only feedback. It is an opportunity to learn. Let the feeling of 'I have started so I will finish' pass. Avoid the idea 'Well I might as well go for a total bender.'

(3) *Review your commitment.* Recall your decision balance sheet matrix. Weigh up the short and long-term benefits of abstinence. Remember how far you have come in the journey of habit change. Do you really believe that a single slip cancels out all the progress you have made to date? Renew your motivation and commitment.

(4) *Review the situation leading up to the lapse.* What events led to the slip? Were there any early warning signals? What was the high-risk situation? You may get new information concerning sources of stress in your life. There may be thoughts and feelings that the effects of the drug taken during the slip are going to overpower you and make it impossible for you to regain control.

(5) *Make an immediate plan of action for recovery:*
- Get rid of all drugs/alcohol.
- Remove yourself from the high-risk situation. Take a walk, leave the scene.
- Plan a substitute activity that will also meet your needs at the moment.

(6) *Ask for help.* Make it easy for yourself. Ask friends or relatives. Telephone the relapse helpline.

Coping with panic

We deal in great detail with coping with anxiety in Chapter 3 of this manual.

Coping with anger

Depression and anger are feelings that pose risks to relapse. Here is our advice to clients who find that anger is leading them into rows (interpersonal situations) and confrontations.

(1) Express it in words rather than actions.
(2) Get rid of the feelings through exercise.
(3) Hit something safe such as a cushion.
(4) Distract yourself:
   • Go shopping. Buy something.
   • Go to the cinema/theatre/museum/art galleries/library. Watch a video.
(5) Practice relaxation techniques. Slow down and control your breathing. Play a relaxation tape.

Coping with craving

General principles
(1) Most clients experience cravings, and many find them difficult to cope with. Cravings vary in intensity and frequency: they may range from a fleeting feeling to pacing around for hours totally dominated by feelings and thoughts about the substance or behaviour.
(2) Many clients report having cravings years and years after the addiction has been controlled. Some ex-drinkers still have a craving 20 years later, but when you ask them what the cravings are like and how often they happen, it becomes clear that they are not very intense and happen about once a year.
(3) Clients will have heard tales of never-ending cravings and can feel despondent as a result. The idea of years of having to cope can be a very depressing thought. It is important to put cravings into some kind of perspective and to tell clients that cravings, in general, slowly become less *frequent* and less *intense* over time.
(4) It is important to work out ways of coping with cravings, otherwise there may *not* be years stretching ahead. Find out what techniques clients have already used in the past, and add in the suggested techniques that we have evolved.

Craving triggers
The other angle to tackle with regard to cravings is to try to find out what triggers them. This can alert the client to either avoid it or prepare for it.

The only reliable way of finding out what triggers cravings for each client is for them to monitor themselves. Monitoring needs to be done over a period of many weeks or months to give enough information to find trends and tendencies and patterns.

The client should keep a diary of every craving, with some information about how severe the craving was, how long it lasted and what was happening just before the craving started. Clients aiming for an abstinent regime would use a craving diary. Clients aiming for a controlled use, e.g. controlled drinking, should keep a drinking diary.

In practice an extensive diary is difficult to obtain. It helps if you can give out craving diaries *before* the individual or group sessions start, say at the assessment interview or during the first group.

Craving diary

It can be difficult to get clients to fill in diary sheets, so it is essential to emphasise the importance of homework assignments. Often the sheets are filled in very poorly with little information. Ask clients to fill in as much information as they possibly can (Fig. 4.6).

It can often be difficult to find trends in the situations which have triggered cravings. Sometimes this is because there are not enough data to go on; sometimes it is because the triggers are at a much more detailed and subtle level than is easily looked at with the diary, for example a feeling of being out of control, or a particular sequence of thoughts. At other times, the triggers are on a larger scale and the therapist may need to focus in and out in order to determine the triggers. When the triggers are on a larger scale there is usually a small, local trigger as well.

For some clients there are so many different triggers to cravings that it is difficult to find any consistent trends, despite many examples.

Craving pack

Learning about cravings does not always help clients cope with them. The aim of our techniques is to help the client cope with the craving at the time it is happening.

The 'craving pack' is a set of individually worked-out instructions, of things to do in a *craving attack*. These can be worked out either in the context of a group or in individual sessions. It is very important to work out the components in the session as individuals rarely have the mental energy to be creative while they are craving. When each client has worked out their own craving pack, they write this out on an index card so that it can be carried around with them (Fig. 4.7).

CRAVING DIARY

Soon after you acted on your decision to put a stop to your addiction, it is likely that you experienced cravings for it again. For many people these cravings are very difficult to cope with and seem to happen out of the blue. What we would like you to do is to learn about your own cravings and to find out what sets them off. To help you do this we have prepared some sheets that we would like you to fill in every time you experience a craving. If you feel as if you are always craving, fill in the diary for times when the craving gets worse.

On the diary sheets there are headings with spaces to fill in. One of the headings is 'strength of craving' and in this section we want you to rate how strong the craving was on a scale of 0–10. When the craving is the strongest you can possibly imagine put 10 and put 0 when there is no craving at all.

It is important to put as much detail as you can manage in the boxes. If you have any questions about the diary sheet please contact your counsellor or group leader.

Craving diary			
Craving	1	2	3
Date/time it began			
Brief description of situation			
Mood at time it started			
Strength of craving (0–10)			
How long craving lasted.			

Fig. 4.6. Craving diaries.

My cravings

(1) How many cravings have you had?   . . . .

(2) On average how often are they?   Every   day/week/month

(3) Divide the cravings into those with a rating of less than 4, those with a rating between 4 and 7, and those 8 and over. Count how many there are in each category.

    Cravings rated less than 4   . . . .
    Cravings rated between 4 and 7   . . . .
    Cravings rated 8 and over   . . . .

(4) If the diary has been filled in for over 6 weeks, divide the diary into 3 or 4 week chunks and work out (1), (2) and (3) for each section, to see if the cravings are getting easier or less frequent.

Section 1
Number of cravings   . . . .
On average, cravings every   day/week/month
    Cravings rated less than 4   . . . .
    Cravings rated between 4 and 7   . . . .
    Cravings rated 8 and over   . . . .

Section 2
Number of cravings   . . . .
On average, cravings every   day/week/month
Cravings rated less than 4   . . . .
Cravings rated between 4 and 7   . . . .
Cravings rated 8 and over   . . . .

Section 3
Number of cravings   . . . .
On average, cravings every   day/week/month
Cravings rated less than 4   . . . .
Cravings rated between 4 and 7   . . . .
Cravings rated 8 and over   . . . .

(5) See if the cravings come in clusters or if they are evenly spread. Clusters/Evenly Spread/   . . . .

(6) Women only: see if there are more cravings pre-menstrually or around ovulation
Pre-menstrually   yes/no
Around ovulation   yes/no

continued

Fig. 4.6. Craving diaries.

(7) Put a tick next to the moods listed below for every time you were in that mood just before the craving began. Put 2 ticks if the mood was particularly strong. There are 2 spaces for any mood that is not listed.

Angry	Lonely
Disappointed	Hassled
Guilty	Embarrassed
Confident	Bored
Elated	Irritable
Tired	Anxious
. . . .	. . . .

(8) Go through the situations, and write down the name of anyone who appears more than twice as a main character.

. . . .
. . . .
. . . .

Put a tick by any of the names above if you think this wasn't just a coincidence.

(9) Put a tick for each craving next to the places/situations where it began.

Work	Home
Travelling	Socialising
Hobby	Unfamiliar places
Talk about substance	Direct contact with
. . . .	substance
. . . .	. . . .

(10) Is there anything else that the situations have in common?

. . . .
. . . .
. . . .
. . . .

Fig. 4.6.   Craving diaries continued.

Session on craving pack

'What I'd like to do in this session is think about ways to cope when you are craving. Hopefully you won't have to use this very often, but it helps to be prepared. We are going to work out some things that you can do when you are craving that will help you ride through it. Can you remember what it feels like to be craving?!'

Craving pack

(1) Recognise the craving.
(2) Brief relaxation techniques.
(3) Positive self-statements.
(4) Distraction.
(5) Much later, when the feelings have subsided, try to work out what the triggers were that set the craving off and note them in the craving diary.

Fig. 4.7. Craving pack.

Pause for discussion. Write up the clients' comments. Try to draw out three aspects: tension, pre-occupied thought and a need for physical activity.

> 'What we need to do is attempt to counter some of these thoughts and feelings. We have evolved a "craving pack" which begins to counter these to some degree. We'll work through the pack in the order that you would do it.'

(1) *Recognise the craving.* 'First and foremost you need to recognise that you are craving This sounds obvious, but the feelings may creep up on you. It is important to stand back from yourself and observe yourself. If you aren't very aware of your moods and feelings then it is important to begin teaching yourself. (One way to do this is to set a watch with a bleeper to go off several times a day. When the bleeper is turned off, the wearer has to examine his or her thoughts and feelings.) Once you can say to yourself "I'm having a craving" you are in a position to do something about it, because you're acknowledging the problem.'

(2) *Brief relaxation techniques.* 'The first thing to do is to take a little bit of space and calm down. To do this you need a brief relaxation technique, one that only takes a few seconds or minutes, like the one that we do at the end of the group. I have two suggestions that we can try out now.

'The first one I call the sand image. Try it now with your eyes closed. It works without them closed but you need to be staring at something bland and uninteresting – unlike me! – so close your eyes. Now imagine that you are made of glass and you are full to the top with sand, a sort of human egg-timer. Now imagine that you have holes at the end of your hands and feet and that the sand is slowly pouring out. Just watch the sand slowly flowing out until its all gone.'

Discuss how this felt.

'The second one I call heavy breathing! Again close your eyes. Now I want you to think about the air that you are breathing in. I want you to watch the air as it goes up through your nose, down your windpipe and into your lungs. Follow the breath back out again. With each breath I want you to watch the air as it flows gently in and out. Try to notice the sensation of the air flowing in and out. Just stay watching until you feel like reawakening.'

Discuss how this felt and which technique they prefer.

(3) *Positive Self Statements.*   Next you need to say something to yourself which counters the good thoughts about alcohol/drugs/food, etc. The things that you say to yourself should not be too complicated and they should remind you of the positive things that you are getting by not using. What can you think of to say to yourself that will help you?'

Write out phrases on an index card; try to get each client to have two or three phrases. Great care has to be taken over the nuances and implications behind the phrases. Here are a few guidelines to help you:

- Self-statements where the client is stopping for someone else don't work very well. Try to change these around to something they want themselves.
- Try to balance the 'shock, horror' statements with positive outcomes; that is, memories of awful things that have happened need balancing with notions of feeling healthier, etc.
- Some self-statements have a punishing 'if-I-don't-do-it' side to them, which should be avoided.
- Clients should believe their own statements.
- Some people find the use of phrases false and unconvincing, for them it is better to evolve images of scenes or memories which are pertinent.
- Many statements have associations for the client which might counter the original intent, or the statement can be said in a different tone internally which either changes its meaning or makes it ironic. For each statement ask yourself the question: 'If I was in a different mood how else might I interpret this?' For example, 'I've lost everything through gambling' might have two possible associations: either 'I don't want this again' or 'I've nothing else to lose so I might as well carry on. I've survived thus far.'

'The process so far is to recognise the craving, do a brief relaxation technique and then say your positive statements to yourself. It often helps if you say them through two or three times.'

(4) *Distraction.* 'After this you need to find something to do to use up some of your frustrated energy and to distract you from the craving. Whatever you choose to do needs to be something that is very absorbing mentally and takes all your concentration. Many people find that physical activities are better at doing this than sedentary ones. The activity also needs to be interesting to you and enjoyable. It helps if the activity lasts for a reasonable period of time – half an hour plus. Watching television usually isn't the solution!'

Clients must have spent hours trying to distract themselves in the past. Ask what they have done that has worked and what hasn't worked.

Ask each client to write out his or her own craving pack on index cards.

'Finally, when you are through the craving, sit down and try to work out what set it off and write it down in your craving diary.'

Coping with depression

We found that depression is the commonest negative emotional state that precipitates lapses/relapses. In our programme we devoted a session to dealing with depression. We used a cognitive/behavioural approach that looks at depression in terms of negative thinking and errors of thinking. The techniques and strategies of dealing with these thinking errors are covered in Chapters 3 and 5.

Use of alcohol-sensitising and other drugs in high-risk situations

The drugs we have used with problem drinkers are disulfiram (Antabuse) and calcium carbimide (Abstem). We have also started to use naltrexone (Nalorex) with opiate addicts. We will limit our discussion to the use of alcohol-sensitising drugs.

Essentially relapse prevention procedures are used to teach the problem drinker to use Antabuse or Abstem in anticipation of high-risk drinking situations (Peachey and Annis, 1985). We used these drugs as a temporary measure for some clients on the relapse prevention programme. It is an assumption that in problem drinkers these drugs reduce both the frequency and intensity of decisional conflict about whether or not they should drink.

Working with clients
- We draw up a hierarchy of anticipated high-risk situations.
- We discuss varying coping strategies.
- One of the coping strategies is the short-term use of Antabuse/ Abstem.
- Clients are encouraged to carry the drugs on their person with a drug card.
- In practice less than a quarter of the clients who carried the drugs used them. All reported that having this as a coping device helped them

Clinical example
A 39-year-old man presented to our unit after two weeks in hospital. He had been admitted via the Accident and Emergency Department because of haematemesis (vomiting blood). He was a daily drinker for 17 years with a very strong family history of alcohol problems. He was temporarily staying with his sister, a pub landlady, to recuperate. He then planned to return to his flat which he shared with a drinking friend. His sister had booked him on a family holiday to Spain for two weeks (all of the family group were drinkers). This was his first experience of abstinence.

In the interview with him we asked him what were low, medium or high-risk situations in his daily activities. We also asked what he could anticipate in the next two weeks as high-risk situations.

Initially he identified family meals when some of the party were drinking. After some discussions with us he became aware of other high-risk situations:

- Living in a pub.
- Going back to live with a drinker.
- The family holiday in Spain.

He agreed that on the holiday *he would most probably relapse*.

Our co-operative management plan
We asked him to suggest strategies to deal with high-risk situations. At this early stage of treatment 'avoidance' is often the most useful strategy.

He agreed to commence a relapse prevention group with us on return from his holiday.

We suggested Antabuse cover as strategy while on holiday. This would be supervised by his sister and we would see him in the week prior to his holiday to check on side effects etc. The use of Antabuse would cease on his return, except as cover for high-risk situations in the future if he so desired.

A group on high-risk situations

A sample session timetable is given in Fig. 4.8.

SESSION TIMETABLE
HIGH-RISK SITUATIONS

Aims of the session
- To define what high-risk situations are.
- To identify each client's current hierarchy of high-risk situations.
- To review what their past and current coping strategies are.
- To review their pre-group homework task, and to anticipate future high-risk situations.

Time	Objective	Content/activity
9.15 AM	Open forum	Minutes of last group. Feedback on how clients have progressed over last week.
9.25 AM	High-risk situations	Brainstorming on the flipchart on what are high-risk situations for all the clients. They can use the information from their pregroup homework (see notes).
9.55 AM	Definitions	See notes.
10.15 AM	Coffee break	
10.30 AM	Coping with high-risk situations	Clients can use their pregroup homework information (see notes).
10.55 AM	Homework tasks	
11.00 AM	Relaxation exercise	See previous group on anxiety for description of exercise.
11.15 AM	Form filling Handout on high-risk situations	Weekly rating scale. Feedback questionnaire.

Fig. 4.8. Session timetable: high-risk situations.

Notes

Extract from a group
In a flipchart brainstorming on high-risk situations clients felt that the
following situations put them at risk:

Lunchtime between work bouts	Overwork
Parties	Pressure from others
Visitors	Holidays
Functions	Families
Conferences	Fatigue
Inadequate	Guilt
Stress	Celebration
Bereavement	After arguments
Depression	Old drinking partners
Lack of balance	Being alone
Sense of loss	Facing decisions
Work situations	Boredom
Thirst	Habit
Frustration	Anger
Cravings	Bad news
Entertaining	Feeling the 'odd one out'
Travelling	Insecurity
Feeling low	Lack of willpower
Meeting people you don't know	

We then grouped these ideas under the general headings of:

- Personal feelings (intrapersonal situations).
- Confronting situations (interpersonal situations).
- Pressure from other people (social pressure).

Definitions
We defined a high-risk situation as any situation which poses a threat
to the individual's sense of control and increases the risk of potential
relapse. A typical handout on high-risk situations is given in Fig. 4.9.

HIGH-RISK SITUATIONS

- Family party/gathering.
- Going to work.
- Conflict (arguments and aggression).
- Celebrating.
- Visiting parents/family (unsorted problems).
- Feeling low/depressed.
- Meeting people you don't know.
- Burned up by pressure at work.
- Socialising with colleagues after work.
- Meeting friends.

CATEGORIES OF HIGH-RISK SITUATION

- <u>Intrapersonal.</u> Feelings and thoughts about yourself, not involving others.
- <u>Interpersonal.</u> Situations involving yourself and a significant person.
- <u>Social.</u> Peer pressure; yourself and other people.

WAYS OF COPING

(1) <u>Intrapersonal:</u>
 - Identify reasons for feeling low.
 - Positive thinking/statements.
 - Seeing other people/friends.
 - Treating yourself.
 - Valuing yourself.

(2) <u>Interpersonal:</u>
 - Get out of the situation.
 - Change tactics.
 - Be assertive.

(3) <u>Social:</u>
 - Avoidance.
 - Plan ahead.
 - Find excuses.
 - Enlist help from friends.
 - Practise ways of coping.

Fig. 4.9. Handout on high-risk situations.

Coping with high-risk situations
We took examples of all three types of situation from the clients' pregroup homework. For example:

High-risk situation: going out with friends whom you know will be drinking.

Coping strategies:

- Run through the situation in your mind – *prepare.*
- Make sure your partner knows you won't be drinking.
- Inform your friends you won't be drinking.
- Decide what non-alcoholic drink you will drink (orange juice, grape juice).
- Keep your glass full.
- Tell yourself 'I won't drink', 'I'll be ill if I drink', 'No drink – no hangover.'
- Think of those close to you, e.g. your family.
- Practice relaxation techniques when tense.

We discussed the importance of being prepared and trying different methods of coping. Also to tell yourself 'Well done!' when you have coped with a high-risk situation successfully.

References

Annis, H.M. and Davis, C.S. (1988) 'Relapse Prevention'. In R.K. Hester and W.R. Miller (Eds) *Handbook of Alcoholism Treatment Approaches.* Pergamon Press, Inc., New York.

Crewe, C.W. (1974) *A look at relapse.* Hazelden Foundation, Minn.

Donovan, D.M. and Marlatt, G.A. (Eds) (1988). *Assessment of Addictive Beavhiors.* Guilford, New York.

Gossop, M. (Ed) 1989. *Relapse and Addictive Behaviour.* Tavistock/Routledge, London.

Marlatt, G.A. and Gordon, J.R. (1985). *Relapse Prevention Maintenance Strategies in the Treatment of Addictive Behaviors.* Guilford Press, New York.

Peachey, J.E. and Annis, H. (1985) 'New Strategies For Using the Alcohol Sensitizing Drugs.' In C.A. Narango and E.M. Sellen (Eds) *Research Advances in New Psychoparmacological Treatments for Alcoholism* Elsener Science Publishers B.V. Biomedical Dussim.

Chapter 5

Thinking Errors

The way someone thinks about him or herself and the world determines how they approach their addictive behaviour and problems of living in general. Some styles of thinking, attitudes and beliefs can facilitate the process of change while others can be a serious block in the path of change.

There has been a 'cognitive' revolution in psychological therapies over the past ten years, where the importance of styles of thinking, attitudes and belief systems has achieved prominence. Many of the ideas underpinning cognitive approaches are incorporated into the relapse prevention model. We outline in this chapter a series of selected ideas from cognitive therapies that we used in our programme.

Some readers might find it useful to read more generally about cognitive-behavioural approaches to therapy. We include some suggested reading at the end of the chapter.

Construction of an internal model of the world

This is an idea proposed by some cognitive theories, such as the personal construct theory (Kelly, 1955). Simply, they suggest that everybody builds up an internal model of how the world, people and him or herself works. This model is then used to understand/explain events and to make predictions. It is assumed that the model is continually evaluated and adapted in the light of new experience. Unfortunately, many people show rigidity or slowness in changing their internal model. For example, a woman who believes that men are not to be trusted and are only after her for sex may meet a man who does not attempt to make love with her on a date. She may change the belief she holds about men. On the other hand she may stick to her belief and attempt to explain the new experience in a number of ways: 'he is probably gay', 'he is after my money', 'I am not attractive to men', etc.

An internal model leads to predictions of how things might work out, which is useful. Unfortunately, these predictions can also affect the situation, becoming 'self-fulfilling prophecies'. A self-fulfilling prophecy (Festinger, 1964) is when a person believes something will happen, and the belief subtly influences the situation to make it happen. This can take place completely outside of the persons awareness. This is particularly seen in addictions, when people have experienced a great deal of failure in trying to change their behaviour. In subsequent challenges the person is plagued by self-doubting thoughts and may not put in the same emotional and intellectual effort. The self-fulfilling prophecy means that a person's model of the world is, to some extent, self-perpetuating.

Some beliefs, attitudes and concepts are more fundamental or central to an individual's internal model than others. These are described as core beliefs (Bannister and Fransella, 1986). Core beliefs are traditionally approached by psychodynamic methods. There is now growing evidence to show the effectiveness of cognitive-behavioural therapies in modifying people's core beliefs (Rachman and Willson, 1980, Beck, 1988).

Much note has been given to self-talk in many cognitive theories (Meichenbaum, 1977, Beck, 1976). This is described as the continual internal conversation that people have. Much of our self-talk happens automatically. For example, when a student got a poor mark for an essay, her automatic thoughts were: 'I've failed. This is all a waste of time, I might as well give up this course.' It is assumed that these thoughts reflect the underlying conceptual structure, such as 'a single failure predicts subsequent failure'. Beck (1979) proposes that negative feelings are consequences of thoughts/cognitions arising from a depressing, pessimistic, etc., conception of the world. Cognitive therapy aims to increase the individual's awareness of the internal world, and change 'maladaptive' internal models by questioning beliefs and assumptions, examining automatic thoughts and testing these through behavioural experiments.

Ways of changing the internal model

Most psychological therapies aim to alter a client's internal model of the world so that problems that have arisen as a consequence of that model are ameliorated. For example, an 'interpretation' that a client avoids close relationships is an observation, probably, about a core belief. The statement is made in the hope that by making this belief overt the client will re-examine the efficacy of it. Most beliefs are unspoken rather than overt.

A cognitive approach tries to teach the client to both elicit assumptions and beliefs and to examine their efficacy for him or herself. This involves raising awareness of automatic thoughts and developing a questioning attitude to these. This is a difficult task for clients as it involves continuous vigilance on their behalf. Structuring this task via a recording form helps impose a simple discipline on the process and enables the therapist and client to work together with 'as live as possible' material. When a client is aware of his or her thoughts, he or she learns to ask questions about them, such as:

- 'Where is the evidence for that?'
- 'What other explanations are there?'
- 'What would you think if you were him?'

By asking this kind of question the client tries to acquire a more objective viewpoint concerning the situation in hand and eventually a less personally destructive internal model. At times simply questioning the objectivity of the thoughts does not lead to any change or there is not sufficient information to challenge them. When this happens a behavioural experiment can often be set up, for example, a client who felt he was not interesting to talk to set up such an experiment. First we decided what signs he could pick up to detect if he was boring; he then observed other people's behaviour towards him in five situations that he knew he was going to be in over the next week. Obviously, in this sort of 'experiment' the client runs the risk of discovering that he or she *is* boring. However, if there is a real problem skills training can be brought into play.

When clients are doing this sort of exercise, 'thinking errors' (distortions in the way information is collected or remembered and generalities deduced) come to the fore. Several authors have produced lists of typical 'cognitive distortions' and the rational-emotive school have lists of typical faulty beliefs (Beck, 1979; Ellis, and Gregory, 1977). The lists can never be inclusive, but they are a useful guide for therapists. These are some of the kinds of distortions or faulty beliefs you would be likely to come across in the addictions field:

- All or nothing thinking: you look at things in absolute, black-and-white categories.
- Overgeneralisation: you view a negative event as a never-ending pattern of defeat.
- Mental filter: you dwell on the negatives and ignore the positives.
- Discounting the positive: you insist that your accomplishments or positive qualities and achievements 'don't count' or 'anyone can do them'.
- Jumping to conclusions: (A) mind reading – you assume that people

are reacting negatively to you when there is no evidence for it; (B) fortune telling – you arbitrarily predict that things will turn out badly.

- Magnification or minimisation: you blow things up out of proportion or you shrink their importance inappropriately.
- Emotional reasoning: you reason from how you feel: – 'I *feel* like an idiot, so I must really be one;' or 'I don't *feel* like doing this so I'll put it off.'
- 'Should' statements: you criticise yourself or other people with 'shoulds' or 'shouldn'ts'; 'musts, 'oughts' and 'Have tos' are similar offenders.
- Labelling: you identify with your shortcomings – instead of saying 'I made a mistake', you tell yourself, 'I'm a jerk' or 'a fool' or 'a loser'.
- Personalisation: you blame yourself for something you weren't entirely responsible for, or you blame other people and overlook ways that your own attitudes and behaviour might contribute to the problem.
- Linking unconnected events: you link things together as though they had the same cause because they either had people in common, happened close together or had an object in common.
- Believing:
  Everyone has to like me.
  I have to do everything perfectly.
  I have to like everyone.
  I shouldn't show my feelings.
  It has to go right first time.
  I mustn't look stupid at all costs.
  I must give 100 per cent to everything.
  Etc.

Notes for therapists

Refer to the session timetable given in Fig. 5.1.

Note 1
When filling in the record form (Fig. 5.2) the clients should describe the situation briefly, answering questions such as what was happening? who was there? what were you doing? and giving any important background information.

It is important that they write down what they were thinking and feeling at the time, not later but at the time. This is quite difficult to do.

SESSION TIMETABLE

THINKING ERRORS

Aims of the session
- To raise awareness of thinking processes.
- To try to identify ways of increasing objectivity, particularly in social situations.

Time (minutes)	Objective	Content/activity
15		Open forum and homework review.
10	Orientate to concept of distorted thinking	Therapist talk introducing ideas of automatic thoughts and distorted perceptions of the world. Brief discussion.
5	Learn to use	Therapist works through record form (see note 1).
10		Therapist uses group members' example with record form – flip chart.
5		Brainstorm alternative interpretations.
15	Adapt to 'real' situation	Role-play situation (see note 2 for examples).
		Ask group what each character might be thinking; what positive or objective thoughts they might have.
15	Learn coping strategies	Brainstorm mental tricks (see note 3 for some examples).
15	Adapt to 'real' situation	Role-play situation (from note 2). Try to use coping strategies.
Allow		
10	Extra discussion	
10	Coffee break	
10	Relaxation exercise to end session	

Fig. 5.1. Session timetable: thinking errors.

RECORD FORM			
Situation	Feeling	Thoughts	Other interpretations

Fig. 5.2. Record form.

Most people record what they would like to have done or their feelings, rather than the thoughts they were having. The thoughts are usually a little blurred in memory as they tend to run in chains or sequences. Even if the client can't remember the whole sequence they should try and write down any phrases they can.

Note 2

Below are two examples of role-play situations:

(1) In the restaurant
Kath, a nervous and lonely middle-aged lady, goes into a restaurant in the early evening when it is quiet. She sits down at a table in the corner so as not to feel too exposed. A young, abrupt waiter comes up to her after only a few minutes and asks her if she is ready to order. She is flustered by this, orders a large gin and tonic to calm herself down and says she will order in a few minutes. The waiter goes away to get the drink and returns after only a short interval. He again asks if she is ready to order. She orders the first thing she sees on the menu and a litre of wine to get through the lonely meal.

(2) Leading a NA meeting (or AA, Gamblers Anonymous, etc.)
Mark was asked to lead the meeting the previous week. He accepted but instantly regretted it. He felt and still feels very flattered by the offer, as leading the meeting is a sign that other people feel that he is now stable enough to be giving things back to the community. Mark feels that he is a cheat because he had a rough week and almost used.

He is also nervous at the idea of sitting in front of everyone, and afraid that he will get it all wrong and make a fool of himself. The meeting is roleplayed, and goes without a problem.

Note 3

Often people find it difficult to think of more positive ways of looking at a situation. Here are some ways to make this process easier, but they all need practice:

(1) Try to imagine what you have thought when looking at other people in a similar situation, as in the example of the NA meeting.
(2) Try to think what you would be concerned about if you were doing their job. For example, in the restaurant most waiters are preoccupied with other bits of the job that they have to do.
(3) Imagine what someone you know, who you feel is confident, would be saying to themselves. It is important that this isn't turned around into 'Fred would cope' or 'Josie would know what to do'.
(4) Imagine what a super-confident public figure would say to themselves, for example Batman or Mrs Thatcher! Try to make their statements outrageous and funny.
(5) Debunk the other people so they don't appear so intimidating – imagine them all with cabbages instead of heads, or as they were when they were children but dressed in the (now very large) clothes they are wearing at the time or think how they would look when sitting on the toilet! The last one is particularly good for debunking pompous or authoritarian people because the more pompous they initially appear the more ridiculous they seem sitting on the toilet! Simply, you are trying to remember that the others are human too.

References

Bannister, D. and Fransella, F. (1986) *Inquiring Man: The Psychology of Personal Constructs*, 3rd ed. Croom Helm, London.

Beck, A.T. *et al.* (1979) *Cognitive Therapy of Depression*. Guilford Press, New York.

Beck, A.T. (1976) *Cognitive Therapy and the Emotional Disorders*. IUP, New York.

Beck, A.T. (1988) 'New Advances in Cognitive Therapy'. Behaviour Therapy World Congress, Edinburgh.

Festinger, L. (1964) *Conflict, decision and dissonance*. Stanford University Press, Stanford.

Kelly, G.A. (1955) *The Psychology of Personal Constructs*. Norton, New York.

Meichenbaum, D. (1977) *Cognitive-Behavior Modification: An Integrative Approach.* Plenum, New York.

Rachman. S. and Willson, G.T. (1980) *The effects of psychological therapy.* Pergamon, New York.

Chapter 6

Psychological Traps

Seemingly irrelevant decisions and the rule violation effect are two mental sets or traps that are often seen in the addictions and can cause problems in the struggle to maintain abstinence or self-control. A typical handout on these topics is shown in Fig. 6.1.

Seemingly irrelevant decisions

These were first formally described by Marlatt and Gordon (1985), but are a phenomenon well-known to most people with addiction problems as *setups*. 'Seemingly irrelevant decisions' describes the series of everyday decisions, such as where to eat lunch, what route to take home, whether to visit this friend or that, which lead the client into a situation where it was beyond human powers to resist temptation. The client is unaware or only partly aware of this process and often can only see the influence of these decisions in retrospect. Friends and relatives will often have been able to see the lapse coming, but the client frequently enters the high-risk situation unaware and/or bound by circumstances to continue the course of action. 'Seemingly irrelevant decisions' describes this process in self deception.

A classic example we have seen is a drug user who had not used for two weeks. She was on a methadone reduction programme. Late one night her boyfriend came home with an old friend who used, reputedly occasionally now. Her boyfriend had offered the old friend a bed as he was homeless. She agreed that he could stay if he didn't use in their flat. Within a few days he was obviously using regularly, clearly had a habit and the debris of injecting was lying around the floor. Within a few more days she had had enough of a binge to totally wreck her methadone withdrawal programme and abandon it completely. She in fact said that she simply couldn't resist the easy access to heroin and that anybody else would have used in her position. Clearly in this situation the decision to let the friend stay was a setup.

PSYCHOLOGICAL TRAPS

Seemingly irrelevant decisions

These are more commonly known as setups. Often people make decisions which appear on the surface to be separate from the problem of self-control. However these decisions become a chain of events, which lead to a high-risk situation or such stress that it's 'not surprising' that they gave in. Often people then feel vindicated that they were not really responsible for the relapse or slip, thus eliciting sympathy rather than taking responsibility for their actions. Every person with an addiction must be aware of some of the setups that they have used in the past. List some of the tricks of this kind that you have played on yourself in the past.

Rule Violation Effect

The rule violation effect can relate to anything where you consciously decide not to do something whether this is eating chocolate or drinking alcohol. In addictions rules are usually seen as absolute, with no half measures. This often leads to the presumption that you are either 'in control' or 'out of control'. Many people begin to see a slip as meaning that a total relapse is inevitable. This means that if a slip does occur it is assumed that there is nothing that can be done to rescue the situation. The all-or-nothing thinking ('I might as well be hung for a sheep as a lamb') can produce a feeling of helplessness, which brings about the very thing that you want to avoid.

The decision never to do something ever again, often produces a sense of loss of control over your life. This can then be converted to the feeling that 'someone' is making you endure this, and consequent covert ways of sabotaging the rule emerge.

It also often gets translated into people directly testing out their control over their addiction to see if the rule still needs to apply to them: 'If I can cope with going around all the wine bars, then I must have excellent self-control and can therefore drink again.'

Try to notice if you do this, this week.

Fig. 6.1. Handout on psychological traps.

Many setups are as obvious as this, but a great number are very subtle and involve small everyday decisions. Creating a lot of stress so there becomes an inevitable need for reward is also a kind of setup: this is an example where lifestyle imbalance merges with setups. (Chapter 9 deals with lifestyle balance problems in detail.)

Here is a useful analogy. A man is driving through country lanes, he has driven through them a few times before and because of his sense of familiarity and confidence he doesn't bother to look at his map, but relies on his memory and sense of direction. At each crossroad he comes to he takes the road in the direction of the village that feels right at the time, without referring to the map for an overall route plan. The signposts only give the local villages and not the major towns. After driving for a good while he suddenly finds himself in Setup City. The only route out is at the far side of town, there are roadworks and it is rush hour too! The only sensible thing to do is to stay where he is for a while, until he has the energy to start again.

Although Marlatt and Gordon (1985) describe this phenomenon, they do not discuss why this happens. In our experience we feel that seemingly irrelevant decisions occur most when there has been a change in the client's balance sheet. For example, a client has been working hard and the effort needed to keep to agreed goals seems to grow or the potential future benefits seem to shrink.

If there has been a change in the balance sheet, this may not be acknowledged into a formal decision to go back to the addictive pattern. This could be because of social pressure, the public nature of the attempt to stop, the fear of needing to justify the decision to interested parties or the avoidance of facing up to the long-term irrationality of the decision with the part of oneself which would like to stop (dissonance reduction). If the change in the balance sheet factors is not made conscious, it may be expressed through phenomena such as seemingly irrelevant decisions.

We have found that clients need to become more aware of their own setups. When they 'find themselves' setting themselves up, re-writing a balance helps to make the decision explicit and helps them work out what factors might be influencing them. Some of these might be ameliorated in other ways.

Rule violation effect

The rule violation effect is a psychological trap (described by Marlatt and Gordon (1985) as the abstinence violation effect), that is very prevalent in addictions. The trap arises from the prohibition of the addictive behaviour when someone elects or is forced *never* to do something ever again. It is irrelevant whether this is abstinence from a favourite food because of an allergy or restraint because of a severe addiction. The way the prohibition is interpreted or construed affects its impact. Some people construe the 'never again' rule as absolute, with no room for error and with the feeling that dire consequences will transpire should the rule be transgressed. Clients who are likely to interpret the rule in this way are those who use a lot of black-and-white thinking, or have been brought up in a strict, authoritarian manner. If the rule is interpreted in a harsh, absolute, self-punitive manner, the pressure of this leads to the rule violation effect.

The rule violation effect suggests that the pressure of the rule makes it more likely that a client will have a lapse and that when a client lapses he or she is less likely to prevent the lapse escalating into a relapse.

This happens in three ways, or three 'thought traps':

(1) *Testing personal control.*   This is a readily recognisable process. The rule is seen as a challenge, a marker against which to test the strength of self-control. If the client can control some exposure to the forbidden fruit, then they must be 'alright now' or need a stiffer test. Either way leads into situations more and more difficult to control, until a lapse inevitably happens. Testing personal control can be seen in thoughts such as 'I'll see if I can cope now, I've been straight for two months', 'If I can resist when I meet Ian, then I must be able to resist anything' or 'If I can stop after one cake, then I must be in control of it.' A classic example of this is a client we saw who went around all his old drinking haunts to see if he was strong enough.

(2) *'"They" are making me stop!'*   In this trap the self-imposed rule stops being a decision to change behaviour and becomes something that is being forced upon the client by outside influences. The person who is seen as 'responsible' for this is often the counsellor, the doctor, 'work,' or a partner. They seem to become authority type figures. It then feels '*they* are making *me* stop'. It is therefore 'up to them' to check up and to ensure that the rules are maintained, and 'what they don't see, doesn't matter'.

(3) *'Once I've started I might as well finish!'*   One of the problems with a 'rule' is that once the rule has been broken, that's it! There are no more rules to give further guidance or structure. The proverb 'I might as well be hung for a sheep as a lamb' sums this up: if a client has a drink (or a cream cake) he or she might as well carry on drinking (or eating).

Many people believe that as soon as they've had a drink (more people have this notion in relation to alcohol than any other substance of abuse) they have no control over their behaviour at all and will therefore drink themselves into oblivion. Often this is not as specific as a spoken belief, but there are many people who refuse to look at ways of *stopping* a relapse once it has started. Sometimes this is because they believe a relapse simply won't happen. It is very important to work out ways out of a relapse before it arises. It is difficult to find the energy to work out escape routes or emergency exits at the time, so they must be worked out in advance no matter how unlikely or undesirable a relapse seems.

Notes for therapists

Refer to the session timetable given in Fig. 6.2.

SESSION TIMETABLE

PSYCHOLOGICAL TRAPS

Aim of the session
• To increase awareness of patterns of thinking, such as RVE and SIDs.

Time (minutes)	Objective	Content/activity
10–15	Open forum + homework feedback	
10	To explain SIDs and to discover what members already know	Therapist talk and discussion on SIDs.
10	Discover choice points	Divide into two groups. Each group looks at a different story and decides where there were choice points (see note 1).
10	Relate this to own situation	Go through past two weeks to find set ups (see note 2).
10	To explain RVE and discover what members already know	Therapist talk and discussion.
15	Relate thought traps to members' situations	Therapist to lead discussion on 'three thought traps', and brainstorm ways out (see note 3).
Allow		
10	Extra discussion	
10	Coffee	
10	Relaxation	

Fig. 6.2. Session timetable: psychological traps.

Note 1

(1) Roger's shopping

Roger worked in a busy estate agency. House prices had been spiralling and there seemed to be a never-ending stream of people coming into the office. He tried to get out to the bank to get his money for the weekend and weekend shopping, but he had missed the bank by only a few minutes and the automatic machine had broken down (again!). As he hadn't time to go to another machine then, he decided that he would have to go after work. In the event he had to work until almost seven o'clock on a 'chain-breaking' scheme that needed to be operational within the next two weeks.

As it was Friday he had originally planned to go to Tesco on his way home from work. Because he was feeling so hassled and tired he decided to skip the shopping and get a take-away for tonight. As he lived only 20 minutes' walk through the park, Roger decided to walk home for some fresh air.

As he began walking he remembered that he did not have any cigarettes, so rather than walk through the park he walked up through Camden Town and past the newsagent. He had forgotten that they would not be open this late. He continued walking. After only a short distance he saw an off licence and he went in. As soon as he entered his eyes were drawn to the rows of bottles of whisky. The owner, of course, knew him and said 'Half bottle of whisky?'

Before Roger realised it he had taken and paid for the cigarettes and whisky and was on his way up the road. Feeling a little remorseful, he thought, 'I will only have one drink tonight.'

When Roger got home he sat down straight away to that one drink. Soon the take-away was forgotten and so was the idea of just one drink.

(2) Maggie's reparation

Maggie had been gambling for about fifteen years. She had a family of four: three tall, gangling adolescents and a young daughter of eight years old from her recently dissolved second marriage. She knew in her heart of hearts that the second marriage went to pieces because of her gambling.

She had originally met him at the races, and gambling was one of the things that they had in common, but over the last few years of the marriage he had begun to put his efforts into his own business and he slowly stopped betting.

But Maggie had bet more and more. By the time they were divorced she had run up debts of over £10,000 and her husband refused to pay any of it off for her. She had been coming for help for several months now and she had decided that this time she was not only going to not bet, she was also going to make amends, particularly to her family.

She had already embarked upon her programme of action. First she needed to earn some money. She had got an interview for the following week as a trainee with a firm of share brokers. She had also decided that if she was going to work she would have to organise the household chores and catch up with herself. She had begun by spring cleaning one of the eldest children's bedrooms. This had taken her two days and she felt very proud of her achievement. Next to come were the other bedrooms, decorating the bathroom (which needed wall-papering after the ceiling had been replastered) and the living room and finally the kitchen which was a complete wreck. Meanwhile she was going to keep house as usual for the children and prepare for the interview.

She got the job, but her programme around the house lagged and she also needed money. The decorating seemed too much and she had hired a local firm to do it, but they wanted payment as soon as the job was finished. Unfortunately the bill arrived before her first month's pay cheque, and this was already spent on household basics anyway. By the time she got her wages she was being hounded, yet again, for money. This time she thought that she would be sensible so she bought some shares that were 'a sure thing' for a quick return!

Note 2

Split the group up into groups of three or four. In each small group each person has to go through their diary of the past two weeks and look for occasions when they had suddenly found themselves in a situation where it was extremely difficult to resist drinking (etc.) or times when the urge to drink or use 'just happened'. Each group goes through each person's diary in turn, identifying how they had set themselves up and what other options were available.

When the groups have finished, reassemble in a large group again. The leader writes up on a flipchart what setups each group has found that they use, then goes through each type of setup and asks everyone to indicate if they are aware if they have used it. The leader can then do a 'top ten setupchart'.

Here are a few of the most common types of setups that you are likely to see.

(1) Engineering exposure to addicted substance, often by mixing with other people who have a similar problem.

(2) Setting unrealistically high targets so that failure is inevitable and consolation understandable.
(3) Testing out ability to refuse a drink in difficult situations under the notion of 'if I can cope with X, I know I will be able to cope with anything.'
(4) Making use of alcohol (etc.) contingent upon someone else's behaviour or luck – for example, as long as Mary doesn't drink at home I'll be alright.'
(5) Putting limiting factors on to things – for example, a market-stall holder who claimed all business transactions took place in the pub and therefore he had to go into pubs daily.

Once someone is aware that they are setting themselves up it is useful to get them to do a balance sheet (see Chapter 8) so that they can remake the decision to or not to gamble, drink, etc. It is then clear to themselves and to others what they are doing one way or the other.

Note 3

Get the group to think up some phrases that they can use themselves. When they have a few prepared statements suggest that they make a note of them in their personal records for the course.

Some examples of self-statements to counter testing personal control are:

- 'I want to take this one step at a time.'
- 'There is no point learning to climb on the north face of the Eiger!'
- 'I want to make this as easy on myself as possible'. 'I know I'm winning by each extra day I achieve. I don't need any more proof.'

To counter '*they* are making me stop':

- The most difficult part is to recognise the thoughts and feelings as they are happening, and to be receptive if other people notice first.
- The way out of this trap is to go back to the balance sheet and re-decide whether to continue with this goal. This way the client can own the decision again, which may be different from the one the group leader wants. It re-emphasises the negative parts of the addiction, which might have been minimized in the grief of loosing the addictive substance.

These are a few ideas that group members have had of what to do if a client is having a lapse – to counter 'once I've started I might as well finish':

(1) Phone or contact an 'Anonymous' member.
(2) Phone or contact a friend who understands.
(3) Physically get away or out of the situation for a few days, go and visit someone, for instance.
(4) Fix up appointments at work or home to which you cannot and never do go intoxicated.
(5) Follow a programme of excessive indulgence that does not include the particular addictive behaviour.
(6) Re-read or re-write your balance sheet and make a decision again about whether you wish to stop.
(7) Say to yourself: 'Just because I've had one/a few bets/drinks/chocolate bars/smokes, it doesn't mean I have to have any more. I have had my last one. Is my life worth ruining for this?'

Ask everyone to pick out three ideas that they think they could use. After they have chosen, ask everyone to go through their 'emergency exits' to make sure that they are practical and realistic and that they have worked out in detail exactly what they will do. For example, which 'Anonymous' meeting or member they will contact, who knows about the arrangement for a trip away, or who they will ask to keep a sum of money available to sponsor the indulgence programme. This part of the exercise is done best if all the group members try to find difficulties in carrying out the plans. When everyone has three realistic plans, hand out an index card, already headed 'emergency exits', to everyone and ask them to write out their three plans on the card. Ask everyone to keep the card in their pocket or handbag all the time as a safety mechanism.

Chapter 7

Assertion

Assertion is a skill that many people with an addiction problem feel they need help with. Assertion is the ability or insistence to stand up for one's own rights or opinions while not infringing on the rights of others. Assertive behaviour is needed when there is some conflict of interests, for example creating time for oneself rather than looking after the family. The ability to be assertive is essential for balancing lifestyle.

An individual can respond to conflict situations in one of three ways. These are:

(1) To be passive, fearful and to flee. This may include avoidance behaviour and refusing to recognise or deal with feelings.
(2) To be aggressive, to show anger and fight. This may include a personal attack, using retaliation, pulling rank or condescension and assuming superiority.
(3) To be assertive, self-confident and confront the situation directly.

Every situation is different, and no single way of coping is right or wrong. Each person has to take into account the characters of those involved, the individual's perception of the situation and his or her perceived ability to cope. The first two options can be seen as being the easiest and often the quickest way out of a situation in the short term.

What is assertive behaviour?

Assertive behaviour conveys a sense of one's own self-assurance and respect for the other person. It is about stating one's position clearly and distinctly while the norms of personal space are observed and kept within an acceptable range. Being assertive can be divided into three broad areas:

- Speech.
- Body language.
- Thoughts/cognitive processes.

A person appears more assertive when all the components are used together. Each one will be looked at briefly.

Speech

This is divided into what is being said and how it is being said. What is being said would largely depend on the individual's interpretation of his or her rights. This allows a person to refuse an unreasonable request and to share their own rationale of the situation. Statements should be clear and distinct.

What is being said is important, but how it is said is vital. Inappropriate loudness, threatening and interrupting could be seen as aggressive behaviour, whereas understating the case by being too soft, quiet or hesitant implies submission. If the voice is relaxed, stating the point with appropriate strength of feeling, a person is seen as being assertive and is viewed positively by the listener.

Body language

A person can say one thing but indicate the opposite by incongruent body language – for example, saying 'I am listening to you', but facing away from the person who is talking. Being assertive needs the message and the body language to be co-ordinated.

Body language is comprised of a number of elements, including posture, distance, facial expression, eye contact and gestures. Posture should be relaxed, upright, open and balanced. Being tense and erect will give the impression of being aggressive, while being slumped and closed in will give the impression of submission.

Thoughts/cognitive processes

Cognitive processes such as expectations and beliefs play a large part in how assertive a person is. Expectations of being able to carry out a certain behaviour will affect whether that behaviour is carried out. For example, if a person expects not to be able to say 'No!', he or she is unlikely to try. Similarly, expectations of the consequences of the behaviour are likely to influence behaviour. For example, if you believe that saying 'No!', will result in aggression or rejection you are less likely to say 'No!'.

Assertive behaviour is also closely tied to an individual's beliefs in his or her rights and other people's rights. Some of the basic rights include:

- Expressing oneself.
- Being treated with respect.
- Stating one's needs and priorities.
- Dealing with people without having to make them like or approve of you.

How does assertion link to addictive behaviour?

Research shows that people with addictive behaviours are particularly deficient in assertiveness skills (Miller and Eisler, 1977). This deficiency could be due to individuals never having acquired the skills, or using addictive behaviour to provide the 'Dutch courage'.

We have found that when clients describe situations in which they have failed to be assertive it leaves them with negative feelings, such as anger and frustration. These feelings have acted as high-risk situations for these individuals, resulting in relapse.

Many people with addictive problems have experienced rejection and disapproval, perhaps in close relationships, within employment or by society. Fear of further rejection and alienation may be a block in being assertive.

Assertion is sometimes about getting what you want. Often an addicted person does not feel they deserve having what they want because they perceive themselves as having made such a mess of what they have been offered in the past. For example, a drug addict having had previous help from a rehabilitation programme finds it hard to request help again having relapsed and left the programme.

Notes for therapists

A person can learn and improve on their ability to be assertive, in a similar way to coping with anxiety (see Chapter 3). Some ideas for developing assertiveness skills are outlined below. A typical session timetable is given in Fig. 7.1.

Speech

During our relapse prevention programmes the clients were encouraged to share and participate actively in each group. This improved their self-esteem and lead to improved confidence.

SESSION TIMETABLE

ASSERTION AND DRINK REFUSAL

Aims of the session
- To increase the group's awareness of assertion and how to use it when refusing alcoholic drinks.
- To allow members to role-play 'refusal' situations.

Time (minutes)	Objective	Content/activity
5	Discover what members understand by assertion	Therapist to facilitate group discussion on what individuals understand by assertion. Note down key points.
15	Relate to past experience	Identify situations in past when the members have been assertive; how did they feel and behave?
5		Therapist talk on assertion: voice, facial expression, eye contact, posture, other alternatives.
10	Learn to use	Therapist to lead games: handpushing, 'yes, no'. Give time for discussion following this.
5	Give idea that everyone will need to refuse drinks	Therapist talk: drink refusal includes everyone, difficult to do, ways to help, assertion related.
	Members to realise why they need to refuse drinks	Brainstorm ideas – comfort, reinforcement, commitment to decision of abstaining.
5	To identify situations	Brainstorm possible drink refusal situations.
	To use for role-play	Identify personal difficult situations.
10	Allow exchange of ideas and information	Discussion on how people offer drinks. Discussion on how people refuse drinks.
5	Give good examples to copy	Show video (Horizon) for examples.
25	Opportunity to practise refusing drinks and improve skills	Role-plays – members to be both offering and refusing. Use video for feedback and group appraisal.

Allow
10	Free discussion	
10	Coffee break	
15	Relaxation exercise to finish session	

Fig. 7.1.   Session timetable: assertion and drink refusal.

Exercise: word game

This game involves getting into pairs. One person (the giver) gives the other (the receiver) an item they have on them, such as a pen or a watch, on the understanding that it will be returned afterwards. The giver has to ask for the item back, but can only say 'yes'. The receiver has to refuse to return it saying only 'no'. This game allows the clients to experiment using a variety of voice tones and changes in volume.

The roles can then be changed. As with any games used it is important to de-role afterwards and to check out what issues the particular game brought up for each person.

Body language

Throughout our relapse prevention programme the therapists are very aware that they are often acting as role models for the clients. Being aware of your own body language and the effect it has is very important.

Exercise

We ask clients to identify one person (a public figure) they perceive to be assertive and on whom they could model themselves. Role-play an assertive situation asking the client to act as if he or she is the model in question. It is important for therapists to be very observant so that they can point out and contrast differences in body posture, etc. A video camera and player is an invaluable asset in teaching assertiveness skills. This provides instant and effective feedback.

Thoughts/cognitive processes

We have discussed in previous chapters (see Chapters 5 and 6) how helping the client to think differently can effect the way in which a situation is perceived.

Using the brainstorming method, clients are encouraged to select two or three positive statements and copy them on to cue cards. Some clients have problems in keeping the statements concise and to the point. Group members will then be encouraged to give some suggestions.

The statements may include:

- I have a right to be treated with respect.
- I have a right to refuse a request.
- I have the right to change my mind.

Clients are encouraged to bring an example of a situation in which they wish to be more assertive. With support and suggestions from group members clients can then get their thoughts into a more ordered fashion and determine what points they wish to put over.

A method we have used very successfully to bring all these components together is role-play. The situations have to come from the clients themselves to ensure that they are pertinent. Each client should be encouraged to describe their particular situation, so that the different roles can be played with as much accuracy as possible.

Situations that have been presented include:

- Refusing alcoholic drinks on your birthday.
- Taking back a faulty item to a shop.
- Requesting time off for a dental appointment.
- Having a person push in the queue in front of you.

Apart from the role-plays giving an opportunity for the clients to prepare and practise certain situations in a safe environment, by the use of a video camera and playback facilities the clients have an opportunity to see how they come across.

For some the idea of using the video creates high levels of anxiety. To help alleviate some of the anxiety, the video is discussed in the assessment interview (see Chapter 2). At each group the video is present as part of the setting and we find that after five or ten minutes the majority of clients forget about its existence.

The video feedback always provides clients with valuable insight into their behaviour and speech in a certain situation. The positive points are always heavily stressed and guidance will be given, by both the therapists and the other clients, on how the client could make improvements.

Once the initial embarrassment of seeing and hearing themselves on a television screen has been overcome, the clients find it very valuable and enjoyable. The sessions that included video feedback were always rated highly by our clients in the evaluation.

Homework

The homework tasks for this session involved clients keeping a record of their assertive and non-assertive behaviour. They were asked to identify weaker areas and work on alternative responses. They were also asked to put the session's rehearsals into practice in the following week and to feed back on the outcome at the following session.

References

Alberti, R. and Emmons, M. (1986) *Your Perfect Right*, 6th edn. Impact, London.

Dickson, A. (1986) *A Woman in Your Own Right: Assertiveness and You*, 2nd edn. Quartet, London.

Miller, P. and Eisler, R. (1977) Assertive Behaviour of Alcoholics: A Descriptive Analysis.' *Behaviour Therapy*, **8**, 146–149.

Chapter 8

Decision Making and Problem Solving

Decision making and problem solving are key factors in both the precipitation and the prevention of relapse. This chapter will touch upon the fundamental aspects of decision making and problem solving. There is a vast amount of literature on psychological theories and research in these topics. This is not the place to review that literature; for the reader who is interested in more in-depth knowledge we have included a few key references at the end of the chapter.

In running relapse prevention programmes we have found these sessions to be the most difficult. In general getting the message across about cognitive/thinking processes, in our experience, is the hardest part of relapse prevention therapy. On occasions we have either lost the group or the individual as a result of being too theoretical or being too simplistic. Nevertheless, communicating these ideas is a challenge and we have found that the clearer we became of the basic concepts the more able we were to get the message across effectively. A typical session timetable and handout on decision making and problem solving is given in Figs. 8.1 and 8.2.

We have found that once the basic message is received clients grasp the essentials very quickly. They readily identify with the processes and reveal their particular patterns, strengths and weaknesses in relation to problem solving and decision making.

Much of the difficulty in communicating the workings of cognitive processes can be attributed to the fact that these processes are generally taken for granted or are 'automatic' to the individual. Asking how one makes a decision or solves a problem is similar to the idea of asking a centipede which leg it moves first.

Sometimes clients have found it an absurdity when questioned about how they make decisions or solve problems and on occasions have shown resistance to looking at these processes. In our experience going back to the fundamental workings of the processes has proved to be an

SESSION TIMETABLE

DECISION MAKING AND PROBLEM SOLVING

Aims of the session

- To increase awareness of the processes involed in decision making and problem solving.
- To identify the client's own patterns, strengths and weaknesses.
- To teach new skills to help effective problem solving and decision making.

Time (minutes)	Objective	Content/activity
5	Introduction of the topics	Brief talk by therapist on the relevance of decision making and problem solving to addictions and relapse.
		(People with addictions show deficits in these areas.)
5	Convey the idea that the client is an 'active decision maker' in regard to the addictive behaviour	Reiterate facts such as client making the decision to seek help, to attend the group; to abstain/control etc. To relapse is also a decision!
20	Different styles of decision making	Using flipchart/blackboard describe key features of hypervigilance and defensive avoidance styles. Get group to give examples from their past of such instances.
20	Convey the idea of 'design matrix' (decisional balance sheet)	Describe 'rational style' of decision making (vigilance). Draw a decision matrix.
		Get an example from the group and set the group the task of filling in the blank.

COFFEE

5	Introduce topic of 'problem solving'	Talk about problem solving as a normal aspect of daily living. There are better ways.
5	Identifying client's individual patterns	Discussion on orientation 'set'. Flipchart
10	Introduce stages of effective problem solving	Trainer talk using flipchart.
20	Practical example	Work through a problem selected from the group.
15	Relaxation exercise	
	Homework	Each client to identify a problem and to go away and apply the model that has been discussed, and report back on progress at the next session.

Fig. 8.1. Session timetable: decision making and problem solving.

DECISION MAKING AND PROBLEM SOLVING

We make decisions every waking minute of our lives. Similarly life poses constant problems that need solving all the time. Because of this we take these processes for granted and rarely bother to look more closely at how we do them. This session is aimed at 'tuning in' to these processes.

The relapse prevention approach considers the individual to be an active 'decision maker' in relation to his or her addictive behaviour and not a 'passive victim'. Starting the addictive behaviour, stopping/controlling, relapsing and attending a relapse prevention group are all decisions made by the individual.

There are two patterns of decision making associated with relapse that a person should be aware of. These are:

(1) 'Hot decisions' which are made when an individual is under pressure. 'Panic' decisions made without considering the full range of consequences are when a person's thinking can be described as 'blinkered'.
(2) 'Blaming decisions' are where the individual decides to indulge in the addictive behaviour by shifting the 'responsibility' to other individuals or situations (external factors).
   'Setups' (seemingly irrelevant decisions or SIDs) are a variation of this pattern. These are where a person takes a series of simple decisions to set up a situation that would compel him or her to indulge in the addictive behaviour and that it would require a moral superhero to resist.

The programme encourages individuals to adopt a 'vigilant' style of decision making that involves the weighing up of short-term and long-term positive and negative consequences of decisions. The best way to adopt such an approach is to use a decision balance sheet like the one shown below and write down all the facts associated with a decision. With practice this could be carried out mentally.

Decisional balance sheet

If I decide to ....

The positive consequences		The negative consequences	
Short term	Long term	Short term	Long term

Problems in life generally have more than one solution. Some solutions are better than others. Effective problem solving is finding the best solution to a given problem. Research shows that effective problem solving is a skill that can be learnt. The following steps are recommended for effective problem solving.

(1) Have a positive attitude towards dealing with problems and don't rush into impulsive solutions.
(2) Define the problem for yourself in clear simple terms and if required break it down into smaller steps. Molehills, not mountains!
(3) Generate as many alternative solutions you can think of and if possible get ideas from others as well.
(4) Decide on the best solution by weighing up the pros and cons of all the alternatives available.
(5) Implement the chosen solution.
(6) Check the outcome of your actions to see whether it matches up to the desired outcome. If not, start again by going back to defining the problem.

It has been found that people who are good at problem solving go through such a process automatically. Take a problem you are facing at present and set about the task of solving it by using this process ... that is if you don't use such a process already.

Fig. 8.2. Handout on decision making and problem solving.

invaluable experience to everyone irrespective of being adept or inept in these areas.

Research shows that individuals with addictive problems are particularly deficient in problem solving skills which include decision making (Intagliata, 1978; Platt *et al.*, 1975). There is also evidence that problem solving skills can be effectively learnt by individuals with addictive problems and that these skills are found to be both retained and generalised at follow-up (Intagliata, 1978). There have been recommendations that all treatment programmes for addictive behaviours should include a component on problem solving training.

In essence the whole of relapse prevention can be described as a training in problem solving. The paradox here is that problem solving training is an integral part of the programme. Assisting clients to improve their problem solving skills will increase their ability to effectively solve problems of daily living and utilise other aspects of the relapse prevention programme. Both these processes should reduce the probability of relapse.

Decision making

Everyone makes decisions from the moment they wake up until they go to sleep. Decision making is an essential component of the problem solving process. It is dealt with separately in this chapter because of the emphasis placed on it in the relapse prevention approach. A fundamental assumption in this approach is that the individual is not a *passive victim* of his or her addiction but an *active decision maker* all the way. Therefore the key to 'giving up', 'continuing', 'changing', 'maintaining' and 'relapsing' all lie in the decision making process. They are all decisions made by the individual.

To be included in the programme the client would have made the *decision* to seek help for his or her problem and subsequently to abstain from or significantly reduce the addictive behaviour (decision to stop smoking, stop or reduce drinking, cut down on eating, etc.). Therapists are advised to place maximum emphasis on this and foster the idea of the client as an active decision maker. The main notion to communicate here is that whether they 'maintain their change', 'indulge in the addictive behaviour' or 'relapse' would be a direct result of decisions made by them. These things don't just happen - somewhere along the line a few decisions were made by the person! A good maxim to use here is 'having self-control means having the power to decide'. The quality and type of the initial decision made by clients to change their addictive behaviour (see the balance sheet at the end of this chapter) is considered to have a strong influence on outcome (Allsop and Saunders, 1989).

Decision making in relapse

A simple rational approach to making a decision would be to weigh up the short-term and long-term positive and negative consequences (cost/benefit analysis) of that decision and choose the most beneficial/least costly path. It may not surprise the reader that decisions associated with lapses and relapses are found not to be carried out in such a cool and calculating manner.

A more appropriate model to help understand decision making in the relapse process comes from the work of Janis and Mann (1977). In their conflict model of decision making they propose five decisional coping patterns that are determined by the level of stress associated at the time.

Low levels of stress are seen as conducive for a cool and calculating pattern, whereas higher levels of stress give rise to different patterns. In decisions associated with relapse there are two factors that may increase an individual's stress levels:

(1) Stressful situations (high-risk situations) that push the individual to a point of decision.
(2) The conflict 'to indulge/not to indulge' does in itself cause increased stress to the individual.

Out of the five decisional patterns described by Janis and Mann (1977) only three are discussed here because of their particular relevance:

- Hypervigilance.
- Defensive avoidance.
- Vigilance.

The first two are discussed because of their relevance to the relapse process and the third because of its relevance to problem solving.

Hypervigilance
This way of thinking is best described by its most extreme mode, the 'panic' response. This is the pattern of frantically searching for a way out of a dilemma, looking for an impulsive/quick solution for immediate relief.

Because of the high stress levels experienced by the person at the *point of decision* there is a narrowing of cognitive processes (a blinkered approach). The full range of consequences of the decision tends to be glanced over. The cost benefit analysis between short-term and long-term positive and negative consequences (decision balance sheet) tends to be discarded in favour of the short-term benefits. The immediate memory span becomes reduced and the number of choices available to the individual appear to be very limited.

Defensive avoidance

This pattern of decision making will be all too familiar to the experienced therapist in the field of addictions. To minimise the conflict of the decision to indulge in the addictive behaviour the individual attempts to absolve him or herself by shifting the responsibility on to an external factor: 'If it wasn't for my friend upsetting me I wouldn't have binged.'

The individual may use rationalisation or denial to support the decision, which involves distortion of facts. Distortions could involve exaggeration of the benefits of indulging in the addictive behaviour and minimisation of the adverse consequences: 'It would bring me all the confidence I need to handle the situation and then I can stop.'

Seemingly irrelevant decisions (SIDs) or 'setups'

This pattern of thinking is typical of the defensive avoidance type of decision making (also see Chapter 6). It is where the individual sets up a situation to indulge in the addictive behaviour, through a series of decisions which enable them to shift the responsibility or blame. The situation when arrived at would be one that it would take a moral superman to resist. Increasing awareness about 'setups' and instilling corrective/coping responses for them is an important part of relapse prevention.

Vigilance

The pattern of decision making that Janis and Mann describe as vigilance is discussed here briefly as it offers an alternative to the maladaptive patterns described above. This is a pattern whereby the decision maker searches thoroughly for alternatives, gathers all the relevant information in an unbiased manner and makes the decision after appraisal of all the alternatives (decision balance sheet). This rational approach to decision making is the pattern required for rational problem solving and will be referred to again in the next section.

Therapists are advised to encourage the use of the vigilance pattern of decision making not only by showing it as an alternative to the maladaptive patterns but also by using it themselves during the programme.

Problem solving

It has been proposed that psychological health (healthy psychological functioning) is largely dependent upon the ability to cope effectively with the demands of problematic life situations (Spivack, 1973). The term 'problem' is used here to describe any life situation where the individual has more than one alternative solution. This could involve all life situations because there is always more than one way of dealing with any situation. A 'solution' to a problem is the 'process' of selecting the most appropriate response from the available alternatives. This process, which is termed problem solving, is also a learning experience, hence results in 'behaviour change'. Effective problem solving can be looked upon as a 'skill' and, like all skills, could be acquired by appropriate 'training'. The aim of the inclusion of this topic in the programme is to give clients a basic training in problem solving.

Stages of problem solving

In a review of the literature on problem solving and a seminal paper on problem solving therapy D'Zurilla and Goldfried (1971) describe five general stages or cognitive operations that many theorists and researchers agree upon.

Before outlining these stages it must be stressed that these are theoretical generalisations and that individuals may differ widely in the way they go about solving problems. It is also acknowledged that in real life problem solving may not take place in such a stage-sequential manner. There could be considerable overlap between stages; a person may jump to and fro from stage to stage and work on different stages simultaneously (Crutchfield, 1969; D'Zurilla and Goldfried, 1971). Nevertheless, the stages described below, which focus on the key cognitive processes in problem solving, can be seen as a prescription for effective problem solving. They are certainly helpful in organising thinking for training purposes.

The five stages are described below.

General orientation ('set')
Most people have a general orientation or a set of attitudes that decide how they approach or tackle problems. When a bill arrives, putting it away so that it will slip your mind (go away) is an example of this that many of our clients have identified with during sessions. Jumping to impulsive or panic solutions when faced with a problem is another example.

Therapists are advised to get clients to identify their style of approaching problems either by eliciting examples from them or by giving them a problem and asking them to outline how they would go about solving it. Changing maladaptive general orientation to problems is a crucial prerequisite for effective problem solving.

Having identified the client's particular style or orientation it is helpful to give examples of orientations that would facilitate effective problem solving. Listed below are three prescribed styles:

- Accept the fact that problematic situations constitute a normal part of life and that it is possible to cope with most of these situations effectively.
- Make sure that problematic situations are recognised when they occur.
- Inhibit the tendency either to respond on the first 'impulse' or to do 'nothing'.

Problem definition and formulation

Problems in real life do not manifest themselves in a well-defined manner. They are often vague and ambiguous. Research shows that defining a problem in clear, simple, unambiguous terms facilitates effective problem solving (Crutchfield, 1969). Clients should be encouraged to describe (preferably write down) problems in their own language using simple and concrete terms. In a group session this could be done as a exercise using a flipchart or a writing board and getting the group members to clarify in concrete terms an example of a problem generated from the group.

Generating alternatives

This is perhaps the most important step to effective problem solving. Poor problem solvers find little or no alternative solutions to their problems. Their solutions are almost automatic and are generally selected from a very limited repertoire. Hence training people to pause to think of as many solutions as possible should be a key objective of this session.

Teaching the technique of *'brainstorming'* is one of the best ways of communicating the idea that there are always alternative solutions to a problem. This is not only helpful in getting the idea across but also for clients to develop it as a fundamental skill. 'Brainstorming' is used extensively in relapse prevention in the group modality as a teaching method. This was first developed in 1938 as a procedure to facilitate 'idea finding' in group sessions (Osborn, 1963).

There are four basics rules in Osborn's method of 'brainstorming'. These are:

- *Criticism is ruled out.* Judgement about the ideas should be withheld until later. This is to be left for the decision making stage.
- *'Free-wheeling' is welcome.* Clients should be encouraged to open up and generate wild and what could be seen as ridiculous solutions. 'Anything goes.'
- *Quantity is wanted.* It is assumed that the greater the number of alternatives, the greater the number of useful ideas. The principle of quantity breeds quality applies here.
- *Combination and improvement are sought.* This is the process of combining the different ideas before the group and setting the group the task of improving on the ideas before them.

When training clients to 'brainstorm' the therapist should keep these basic rules in mind and give general instructions to encourage the free generation of ideas. For Example: 'there are fifty ways to leave your lover'.

Decision making

Once a list of alternative solutions has been generated a particular solution can be selected using the process of rational decision making (see previous section). By this we mean weighing up the 'pros' and 'cons' of each solution and selecting what promises to be the best available option (decision balance sheet).

Verification (evaluation)

Having decided upon a course of action (solution to a problem), many individuals rarely pause to evaluate the outcome of their actions. Hence it is very important to teach people the final step that contributes to effective problem solving. Without this step there is no opportunity for self-correction and there is the danger of a person persisting with an inadequate course of action. If the individual has selected the right solution verification would result in increasing confidence in his or her ability to successfully solve problems (increased self-efficacy).

The whole of the problem solving process described above can be understood as a feedback loop system. This is best outlined by the 'test-operate-test-exit' (TOTE) unit described by Miller *et at.* (1960). For a given life problem, such as having rent arrears and facing the possibility of eviction, the problem solver has an expected outcome: avoiding eviction and not getting into arrears. After carrying out a selected course of action the individual should test or match the outcome of the action with the expected outcome. If the match is satisfactory the problem solving process is terminated (exit). If the match is unsatisfactory the problem solver returns to the 'drawing board' and goes through all the stages of problem solving (problem definition, generating alternatives and decision making) again. This process is to be repeated until a satisfactory solution is found.

References

Allsop, S. and Saunders, W. (1989) 'Relapse and alcohol problems'. In M. Gossop (Ed) *Relapse and Addictive Behaviour*. Tavistock/Routledge, London.

Crutchfield, R.S. (1969) 'Nurturing the cognitive skills of productive thinking.' In *Life skills in schools and society*. Association of Supervision and Curriculum Development, Washington, D.C.

D'Zurilla, T.J. and Goldfried, M.R. (1971) 'Problem solving and behaviour modification.' *Journal of Abnormal Psychology*, **78**, No.1, 107–126.

Intagliata, J. (1978) 'Increasing the Interpersonal Problem-Solving Skills of an Alcoholic Population.' *Journal of Consulting and Clinical Psychology*, **46**, No. 3, 489–498.

Janis, I. and Mann, L. (1977) *Decision Making: A psychological analysis of conflict, choice and commitment*. Free Press, New York.

Miller, G.A., Galanter, E. and Pribram, K.H. (1960) *Plans and the structure of behavior*. Holt, Rinehart and Winston, New York.

Osborn, A.F. (1963) *Applied imagination: Principles and procedures of creative problem-solving*. Scribner's, New York.

Platt, J.J., Spivack, G. and Siegel, J.M. (1975) 'Do psychiatric patients and normals see the same solutions as effective in solving interpersonal problems?' *Journal of Consulting and Clinical Psychology*, **43**, 279–285.

Spivack, G. (1973) *A conception of healthy human functioning*. Department of Mental Health Sciences, Hahnemann Medical College and Hospital, Philadelphia, Pa.

Chapter 9

Lifestyle Balance

Two underlying assumptions in this relapse prevention programme are that:

(1) Stress of various kinds makes relapse into addictive behaviour more likely.
(2) Relapse may be prevented if either the sources of stress are reduced or one's capacity to cope with them is improved.

The balance between stress and coping mechanisms

How much stress we experience in life depends on two factors:

- The *sources of stress* or life stressors we encounter.
- Our *resources to avoid or cope* with these stressors.

For the purposes of relapse prevention a *balanced lifestyle* implies a balance between these two. We feel stressed, however, when an imbalance exists with either too many stressors or too few resources to avoid or cope with the sources of stress or stressors in our lives.

This dynamic balance is a bit like a see-saw. In Fig. 9.1 the stressors outweigh the repertoire of coping skills, and stress results. In a moment we shall be looking at some different sources of stress but first a couple of examples may illustrate the balance between stressors and coping.

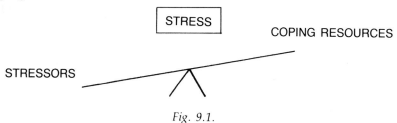

Fig. 9.1.

Examples

(1)   Margaret had always coped with more informal get-togethers with acquaintances of her husband, but when he was promoted and she was required to entertain his boss or potential customers at home she started to drink more alcohol to control her anxiety before these events.

In this case the various skills Margaret possessed to enable her to interact casually with her husband's friends and acquaintances were inadequate to meet the increased demands of having to meet, converse with and cater for her husband's business associates.

(2)   John had always been prone to spells of pessimism and sadness, but his girlfriend Sarah had been a great support to him during these periods and had often been able to give him a sense of perspective or distract him away from his feelings of hopelessness. Since Sarah had left him, however, he felt quite unable to cope with his depressed feelings. He started to take tablets which a colleague at work recommended and could get for John, albeit at a cost. The tablets seemed to give him a temporary lift in his mood, but he found it increasingly difficult to do without them and continuing to buy them from his colleague was becoming a drain on his financial resources.

The loss of Sarah not only meant that John felt bereft and lonely after the separation, but one of his main ways of coping with his periods of despondency had been removed – the facility of talking over and discussing his worries and feelings with her.

Both these examples show how the often tenuous balance between stressors and someone's means of coping with that stress can easily be upset. But what are some of the sources of stress that life may throw up and how can they be classified?

Types of stress

Major life events

Major changes in one's circumstances, or life events, have been studied and an association has been demonstrated between adverse or beneficial life events and many different psychological as well as physical conditions. More often the focus has been on adverse or unpleasant events, examples of which might be marital separation, loss of a job, being involved as defendant in a court case, finding out you have an illness of uncertain prognosis and so on.

Of course finding an association is not the same as proving a causal link and it is often difficult to determine the precise sequence of happenings and how they are related to one another.

Example

At about the time Peter started to take heroin again his relationship with Susan deteriorated. He wasn't quite sure which came first. Susan complained bitterly about his taking the drug and her nagging only seemed to make him take more to blot out how rejected and wretched he felt. Finally she left him. She said it was finding a needle and syringe left within reach of the children which was the final straw. It was at about this time that his habit really became serious and he felt he badly needed help.

So a relapse into heroin use may be due to the breakup of a relationship, with drug use perhaps a way of blotting out feelings of rejection or loss. On the other hand, however, a partner may be antagonised and finally leave because of difficulties from someone's increasing dependence on heroin.

Teasing out the precise order in which things happened can be extremely difficult and, perhaps not surprisingly, determining the exact causal role of life events in research is fraught with problems. Research methods of recording life events have become more sophisticated over the years in attempts to overcome various methodological problems.

Earlier instruments to measure life events (e.g. Holmes and Rahe, 1967) have:

(1) Failed to distinguish sufficiently between life events preceding the condition which are therefore putative causal factors, and those which may have arisen as a result of the condition.
(2) Often inadequately covered the scope of possible life event experience.
(3) Tended to be ambiguous in their definition of events for rating.

Later instruments (e.g. Brown and Harris, 1978) have overcome many of the methodological snags, but this has tended to be at the expense of ease of administration. The methodological issues which make it difficult to be certain about the exact causal role of life events in addiction have been reviewed by O'Doherty and Davies (1987).

Hassles and uplifts

It is possible that the more minor occurrences of daily life, either pleasant or disagreeable, may be at least as important an influence on the course of addictive behaviour as more major life events. Here we are talking about the ups and downs or 'hassles' and 'uplifts' of day-to-day life (Kanner *et al.*, 1981). Examples of hassles might be receiving an unexpected bill, a colleague going off sick at work, or finding after you have arrived for a meeting that the arrangement has been changed. Uplifts might be your child getting a good report from school, accomplishing to your satisfaction a work task, a period of good weather and so on.

It can be seen that the difference between so-called hassles and uplifts and the more major adverse or beneficial life events mentioned above is really one of degree, and there can be overlap in the scope of instruments measuring life events and those recording so-called hassles.

Shoulds and wants

Marlatt and Gordon (1985) have distinguished between activities in daily life perceived as chores or things one feels obliged to do – so-called 'shoulds' – and those activities carried out for pleasure, satisfaction or self-fulfilment – 'wants'. Examples of shoulds might be visiting relatives you feel you have very little in common with, a business meeting or cleaning your home. Wants on the other hand might be going swimming with friends, planning a holiday or watching a particular programme on television.

Shoulds and wants are a subjective judgement; an activity could be a should to one person and a want to another. Often activities will change between a want and a should for someone depending on other pressures and circumstances. In Marlatt and Gordon's model it is the accumulation of too many shoulds that leads to the desire for indulgence. The desire to indulge is dangerous as it can fuel the route to a lapse. We have found that frequently the shoulds build up to a point, or threshold. Once this threshold is reached the desire to throw in the towel and treat oneself is powerful.

When someone's quota of shoulds outweighs the wants a lifestyle

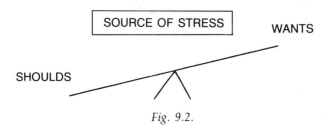

Fig. 9.2.

imbalance arises. Such an imbalance may form an important background source of stress leading to addiction relapse – see Fig. 9.2.

Indeed in the case of substance use a vicious cycle of using different drugs may occur, taking one to counteract the effects of another. Alcohol for instance may be taken as a treat after a period of too many shoulds with too few wants to enliven the situation or relieve feelings of deprivation. Alcohol depresses the nervous system and when taken in excess there is then the temptation to take a stimulant drug such as caffeine in coffee to speed one up again, perhaps to face another day of unrelieved shoulds. After these shoulds alcohol may again be taken as a reward and so the cycle may go on with increasingly harmful consequences.

The shoulds and wants exercise focuses on a micro-analysis of stress in everyday life. Stress can also be caused by an absence of things as well as the presence of demanding situations. The classic example of this is the unfulfilled housewife, where lack of stimulation creates stress. The overall content of lifestyles also needs to be tailored to individual needs. The addictive behaviour fulfils some of these global or overall needs, which then need to be fulfilled in other ways to reduce the chance of the addiction reasserting itself.

Ways of coping

If we turn our attention now to a person's resources to cope with stress, certain of the more *specific* kinds of coping skills are covered in other sessions. These include anxiety management skills (see Chapter 3), social skills (see Chapter 7) and self-monitoring of depressive thoughts (see Chapter 5). However some strategies or belief systems are thought to provide a person with a more general protection against stress arising. The impact of such factors is seen as more *global*, not only improving someone's capacity to deal with stress of different

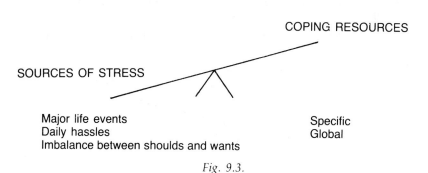

COPING RESOURCES

SOURCES OF STRESS

Major life events
Daily hassles
Imbalance between shoulds and wants

Specific
Global

Fig. 9.3.

kinds across a variety of situations but going beyond that in promoting personal development with enhanced self-esteem and self-fulfilment. Marlatt and Gordon (1985) include among such factors regular physical exercise, relaxation practice, meditation, and having religious beliefs or a spiritual aspect in one's life.

Figure 9.3 summarises the different contributions to the delicate balance between sources of stress and coping resources.

Positive and negative addictions

Some of the global strategies or practices may themselves take on an addictive nature and the term 'positive addictions' has been coined to distinguish such beneficial activities from those 'negative addictions' which this relapse prevention programme aims to counter (Glasser, 1976).

For an activity to become a positive addiction these six requirements should be met:

(1) It is something non-competitive that you choose to do and you can devote about an hour a day to it.
(2) It is possible for you to do it easily and it doesn't take a great deal of mental effort to do it well.
(3) You can do it alone or rarely with others but it does not depend upon others to do it.
(4) You believe that it has some value (physical, mental or spiritual) for you.
(5) You believe that if you persist at it you will improve, but this need only be your belief or opinion.
(6) The activity must be something you can do without criticising yourself. If you can't accept yourself during this time, the activity will not be addicting (Glasser, 1976).

Generally negative addictions tend to have some rewards in the short term but are detrimental to the person in the longer term. To take an example, the more immediate effects of alcohol drinking may include the pleasant taste, a degree of disinhibition which facilitates social interaction and slight intoxication enabling the person to forget temporarily some recent disappointment or more deep-seated problems. Of course the later consequences of a drinking episode may be a hangover or the effects of perhaps loud embarrassing behaviour while intoxicated, and the longer term sequelae of a drinking habit can be problems to health such as gastritis or liver impairment, as well as effects on occupation and the disruption of cherished relationships.

On the other hand positive addictions tend to have beneficial and desirable pay-offs in the longer term after some earlier difficulties have been worked through. For example, for someone not used to physical exertion swimming may initially cause exhaustion and aching muscles. If persisted with, however, regular physical exercise pays dividends in terms of improved physical fitness as well as psychological well-being. The early response to attempting meditation may be boredom or mental restlessness while the effects in the longer term may include feeling more relaxed and self-assured as a person (West, 1987).

Working with clients towards changing lifestyles

Arriving at and putting into practice a programme of lifestyle change may be seen as a journey of mutual exploration and trial between therapist and client. The therapist should be in the role of co-investigator or colleague to the client. The aim is to arrive eventually at a programme which is suitable and individualised for the client. Certain points about working with clients on changing lifestyle are worth mentioning.

Lifestyle change interventions, in this package, are directed at clients who have most of their basic physical needs met. If clients have no home, no money and no food, like some drug and alcohol abusers, then emotional and psychological needs cannot be addressed without first resolving these basic needs. Clients with such impoverished lifestyles need help from social services and housing initially. Once some degree of stability has been achieved the client's lifestyle will need to be built up from scratch. The huge vacuum that the addiction and survival tasks leave is a difficult one to fill. A residential project may be the best place to initiate this process.

Positive lifestyle changes often involve overcoming early difficulties such as boredom or physical discomfort in order to achieve longer term benefits. This aspect of delayed gratification makes it important to assist the client to overcome the initial resistance (see Fig. 9.4). Discussion, with preparation and encouragement, can assist the client to delay gratification and overcome initial resistance until the behaviour begins to provide rewards. These rewards may be specific to the behaviour such as relief of worry and relaxation with meditation or a pleasant feeling of fatigue and afterglow with exercise, or more general in terms of a sense of pride, achievement, increased self-mastery or enhanced health.

Not only may the client need information to carry out certain behaviours, such as learning to meditate, but potential problems should be discussed (setting sufficient time aside for the activity, dealing with the client's and other people's attitudes to the behaviour).

Early goals should be easily achieved and the aim should be to gradually increase the time spent on the activity, its frequency or its

Much too young
to meditate

Too boisterous
to meditate

Too impulsive
to meditate

Too in love
to meditate

Too busy
to meditate

Too tired
to meditate

Too many worries
to meditate

Too old
to meditate

Too late
to meditate

Fig. 9.4.   Such is life. (Reproduced with permission – first published in French in *DHARMA* 4, December 1988.)

intensity. With meditation, for example, an initial goal may be one 10-minute session daily, building up gradually to perhaps two periods each of 20 to 30 minutes every day.

Although Glasser (1976) has emphasised that for an activity to become a positive addiction it should be possible to carry it out alone and it should be non-competitive, the support of others may sometimes be useful not only in helping someone overcome initial inertia until a habit is developed but also in maintaining regularity of the activity.

The behaviour tried should accord with the client's needs and prefer-

SESSION TIMETABLE
LIFESTYLE

Time (minutes)	Objective	Content/activity
10	Discover what group members understand by the term 'stress'	Brainstorm exercise in which group members suggest words or phrases which they associate with stress.
		Therapist writes them on the flipchart. Examples might be: 'pressure', 'too much to do', 'after my best friend got married and moved to the other side of town', 'when my boss out of the blue asks me to do some work urgently', 'after I was transferred to a different department at work'.
15	Describe life events and day-to-day upsets or hassles as two main kinds of stress	Therapist talks about life events and daily hassles as two main sources of stress. The group with guidance from the therapist takes examples of each from the flipchart.
10	Explain terms 'shoulds' and 'wants'	Therapist outlines meaning of 'shoulds', i.e. daily activities perceived as chores, and 'wants', i.e. those activities carried out for pleasure or satisfaction.
20	Clarify role of imbalance between shoulds and wants as a source of stress	See Note 1.

continued

Fig. 9.5. Session timetable: lifestyle.

Time (minutes)	Objective	Content/activity
20	Outline concept of overall needs	See Note 2.
	Analyse unfulfilled areas of need and ways of fulfilling these	
Or		
20	Outline role of global coping strategies as protectors against stress	Therapist leads discussion on global coping strategies which might provide more general protection against stress. Group members describe any such strategies in their lives and the benefits they feel these activities or belief system confer. Examples might be: regular exercise, putting time aside each day for relaxation or meditation, religious beliefs, belonging to an inspirational group such as Alcoholics or Narcotics Anonymous.
	Outline of positive addiction concept	If there is time, therapist may introduce into discussion concepts of positive and negative addictions, particularly how the former often involves some short-term snags or drawbacks before longer-term gains are realised, while it is usually the reverse situation for negative addictions. Examples are sought from group members and discussed.
10	Homework task	Distribution of handouts for next session. Therapist goes through the handout providing any necessary explanation and tries to ensure that all group members understand the nature of the homework task.
10	Free discussion	
10	Coffee break	
15	Relaxation exercise to finish session	

Fig. 9.5.   Session timetable: lifestyle continued.

ences. For instance if the person experiences stress mainly at a cognitive level, such as frequent worrying, and in addition adheres to a religious belief system or is relatively spiritually aware, meditation may be a suitable activity. If someone experiences muscular tension and additionally puts much store by physical appearance and attractiveness, physical exercise with possibly also progressive muscular relaxation may become a rewarding and eventually an habitual activity.

Goals should not be so rigid as to invite failure. A goal that 30 minutes are spent in meditation before breakfast daily may be ideal but someone is more likely to attain goals which are less absolute and allow more flexibility not only as regards timing and time spent on activities but also between different activities. A more suitable goal might be to find time for oneself sitting quietly alone at some time during a 24 hour period. This time might be spent in more formal meditation or in less formal tranquil contemplation.

LIFESTYLE

Stress is an important factor leading to relapse in addictive behaviour. You may already have discovered this for yourself from your own experience. Perhaps you find it more difficult to avoid the temptation of having a cigarette or an alcoholic drink or whatever your form of addiction may be when you feel under pressure.

Stress comes in many different forms. It may be because of a major change in one's life (life event) – e.g. the loss of something valued such as a job, or a bereavement. However, the more frequent day-to-day happenings in one's life also seem to be important in determining how stressed one feels. These daily occurrences may be perceived as unpleasant (hassles) or as ones which cheer you up (uplifts).

The balance between those activities seen as chores or things you feel you have to do – SHOULDS – and those which are pleasant and carried out for fun or satisfaction – WANTS – seems to be an important determinant of your background level of stress.

In the next session we shall be looking at the different kinds of stress people experience as well as discussing those activities which can prevent or counteract stress.

During each day of the next week, on the sheets provided, list the activities you engage in. Please record the following:

(1) The time you begin and end each activity.
(2) A brief description of each activity ('travel to work', 'lunch with two work colleagues', 'went to the cinema with a friend').

Fig. 9.6. Handout on lifestyle.

Write down all your daily activities from the time you wake up to the time you go to sleep, in that order. Mark each activity with an (s) if you consider it a 'should' or a (w) if you consider it a 'want'. Add-up the total number of 'shoulds' and 'wants' for each day.

Date:

Time		Activity		Should	Want
From	To				

Total

Fig. 9.7.   Daily want/should record.

An activity which becomes part of someone's lifestyle in the longer term will be rewarding to that person. If a behaviour does not become reinforcing it will not be persisted with. The former situation stands more chance of realisation if the activity is from an early stage as pleasurable as possible to the individual concerned – or just sheer fun!

Notes for therapists

Note 1: shoulds and wants

Ask the group members to go through their diaries that were given out the previous week and rate each activity as a 'should' or a 'want'. This exercise can't be done using a typical day because often things are shoulds one day and wants another. For example making an evening meal can be a want when there is plenty of time, nice food to cook and cheerful children, but at other times things may be different. Often things change from a want to a should when there is pressure.

Once the group members have rated each activity they should add up their total shoulds and total wants and look at how they are distributed. Ideally shoulds and wants should be spread evenly throughout the week, with some wants every day. It is the build-up of too many shoulds without respite that creates the desire for indulgence. Encourage group members to dot small wants throughout the day – a walk at lunch time, reading etc.

Working women frequently have all their wants at work and all their shoulds at the weekend, such as 'should spend time with the family', 'should get the house tidy', etc. Others may have all wants, especially if they are unemployed and not living with a partner. When clients have an all want pattern it is worth looking at the quality of their wants and relating this to the life needs outlined in the following exercise.

Note 2: 'What I need for a fulfilling life'

This exercise is done by asking the group to brainstorm what things they and others need in order to have a satisfying and fulfilling life. Write these up on a flipchart. Some examples of things that people have come up with are listed below.

Love	Sense of purpose
Companionship	Money
Sex	Fulfilling emotional life
Excitement	Achievement
Routine	Stability
Food and shelter	Risk
Personal space	Respect
Physical activity	
Someone to lean on	

The group members then mentally run through the list to see what factors they feel they have in their lives. Many of the factors are not black or white concepts but are continuums; some people need a lot of personal space while others need very little. Each group member needs to assess whether they have too much or too little of these factors in their life.

This exercise is a macro-analysis of clients' lives. When group members have identified their lifestyle needs, discuss ways of fulfilling these needs. Many hobbies/societies/types of work fulfil a great many of these factors at one time. (You can test this out by asking the group – 'What do people get out of sport?' – a list will be produced similar to the one produced by the question 'What do you get from your addiction?') The addiction has been fulfilling some of these needs that now needs to be met within the client's current lifestyle. For example, heroin use tends to be sociable, provides excitement and risk, structures daily life. This kind of analysis is useful in trying to find the right activities to fill in the spare time the addiction has left.

References

Brown, G.W. and Harris, T. (1978) *Social Origins of Depression. A Study of Psychiatric Disorder in Women.* Tavistock Publications, London.

Glasser W. (1976) *Positive Addictions.* Harper and Row, New York.

Holmes, T.H. (1967) 'The Social Readjustment Rating Scale.' *Journal of Psychosomatic Research*, **11**, 213–218.

Kanner, A.D. *et al.* (1981) Comparison of two modes of stress measurement. Daily hassles and uplifts VS. major life events'. *Behavioural Medicine*, **4**, 1–39.

Marlatt, G.A. (1987) 'Lifestyle modification.' In Marlatt, G.A. and Gordon J.R. (Eds) *Relapse Prevention.* Guilford Press, London.

O'Doherty, F. and Davies, J.B. (1987) 'Life events and addiction: a critical review.' *British Journal of Addiction*, **82**, 127–138.

West, M.A. (Ed) (1987) *The Psychology of Meditation.* Clarendon Press, Oxford.

Chapter 10

Depression

Many people describe returning to an addictive behaviour when they feel despondent or miserable. Indeed systematic surveys of the antecedents for relapse into addictive behaviour have highlighted the important role depression may play (Cummings, Gordon and Marlatt, 1980). Hence our reason for devoting a session to looking at depression (Figs 10.1 and 10.2) and methods of avoiding it or coping with it after it has arisen.

By 'depression' we mean the syndrome or group of symptoms occurring to varying degrees when someone is feeling sad.

Example
When Simon was made redundant he thought at first that being out of work wouldn't be so bad. But suddenly he found he had all this time on his hands and after a couple of weeks there didn't seem to be so much incentive to get out of bed in the mornings. What was more he was finding it more difficult than he had anticipated to find another job and he began to think his friends who still had jobs would not be so interested in seeing him any longer. In spite of getting up later and later he seemed to have less energy rather than more during the day. But perhaps that was connected with his increasing difficulty in getting off to sleep at night. His brother noticed Simon was looking thinner. Simon was beginning to wonder what was the point of it all anyway.

So associated with a lowering of mood may be other features. These include lack of appetite, difficulty in sleeping, lack of interest in oneself and the things going on around one, and pessimistic thoughts concerning one's abilities and effectiveness and what the future holds in store. In more severe instances, feelings of hopelessness about the future may lead to thoughts of suicide. In particular when so called 'biological' features of depression are present some consider that an illness is then present and that antidepressant medication is likely to alleviate

SESSION TIMETABLE
DEPRESSION

Time (minutes)	Objective	Content/activity
10	Discover what group members understand by the term 'depression'	Each group member to say one sentence about their understanding of 'depression'.
		Pick out key words on flipchart.
10	Summarise meaning	Therapist to clarify usual meaning of 'depression', outlining frequent components of the condition.
15	Elicit examples of negative thoughts and explain their relationship to self, environment or future ('negative triad')	Each group member is invited to provide from his or her homework sheets two or three examples of thoughts which were associated with depression. Write these on flipchart and categorise according to relationship of content to self, environment or future.
15	Explain faulty thought processing which can produce negative thoughts and identify some of the different mechanisms	Involve group members in examining some of the thoughts. Take two or three examples on the flipchart. Invite group members to comment on the likely validity of the thoughts. How much evidence is there to confirm or refute them? How could they actually be tested?
		Elucidate the kind or kinds of dysfunctional thinking which could have led to these thoughts.

15		Therapist outlines some of the other types of possible faulty thought processing such as overgeneralisation, personalisation, magnification, minimisation, dichotomous reasoning, arbitrary inference, selective abstraction.
		Invite group members to provide examples from their experience. Lead on to the importance of attempting to scrutinise critically the validity of one's own thoughts.
10	Elicit examples of rewarding activity	Brainstorm exercise for examples of pleasurable or satisfying activities.
		Lead discussion on connection between depression and level and kind of activity. Lead on to strategy of increasing amount of positively reinforcing activity as a means of countering depression.
10	Homework task	Distribution of handouts for next session. Go through with explanation and try to ensure all group members understand the nature of any homework task.
Allow		
10	Free discussion	
10	Coffee break	
15	Relaxation exercise to finish session	

Fig. 10.1. Session timetable: depression.

DEPRESSION

Despondent, depressed feelings often seem to lead to a lapse back into addictive behaviour, be it alcohol drinking, smoking or whatever kind of behaviour the person has been addicted to.

Invariably the feelings of sadness or depression are associated with thoughts of a negative, pessimistic kind. We may begin to think for instance that we are less interesting or attractive people, that other people are unco-operative, unhelpful or overcritical, and begin to be less optimistic about the future.

It is now believed that negative thoughts of this kind actually lead to feelings of sadness and unhappiness and that the ability to recognise one's negative thoughts is important as a means of preventing the emotion of depression occurring or of relieving it once it has already arisen.

In the next session we shall be looking in more detail at how thoughts and feelings may be connected.

Between now and the next session it would be useful to note on the tables provided any situations which give rise to miserable, sad feelings, to rate the extent of the depressed emotion from 1–100, and to record also any thoughts associated with the emotion. Some examples are given on the first page. The situations may be actual events, or may be streams of thought, daydreams or memories.

Fig. 10.2. Handout on depression.

the condition. The biological symptoms are loss of appetite and weight loss, early morning waking (waking in the early hours of the morning with difficulty in getting back to sleep again) and a diurnal variation in mood so that the person feels lowest in mood in the mornings but picks up during the rest of the day.

Some of the more recent ways of looking at depression derive from cognitive and behavioural psychology and techniques based on such theories have been derived to prevent and relieve depression. In practice the treatment of any person tends to use techniques of both kinds but for the purposes of outlining below some of the concepts, cognitive and behavioural approaches will be presented separately.

Cognitive approaches

Traditionally lowering of mood has been considered the primary altera-tion in depression, with the other features of the syndrome arising as a consequence of this. Cognitive therapy on the contrary assumes that mood may alter secondarily to someone's thoughts and that depression may therefore be treated by remedying faulty thoughts and the underlying beliefs from which such thoughts arise.

In depression dysfunction is said to occur in what depressed persons think (their *thought content*), the way they form thoughts (their *thought processing*) and in their underlying attitudes and *beliefs*.

Thought content

According to Aaron Beck, who developed cognitive therapy, the depressed person's thinking is characterised by a triad of negative, self-defeating thoughts about him or herself, the world and the future (Beck *et al.*, 1979), see Fig. 10.3. The person views himself as unattractive, uninteresting or useless, others as unhelpful, critical or overdemanding, and the future as unpromising insecure and threatening.

Thought Processing

Each depressed person has his or her own repertoire of unhelpful kinds of thoughts which habitually spring up – so-called 'automatic thoughts'. Some of the more common examples of the faulty logic producing them are:

(1) *Over-generalisation.* Making a sweeping statement about oneself following a single incident: 'She didn't want to go out with me – that means no-one will.'

(2) *Personalisation.* Attributing failures to oneself when other factors may be at least as much to blame: 'She didn't enjoy the evening at the cinema because she was with me.'

(3) *Magnification.* Misinterpreting a minor setback as a major disaster, 'making a mountain out of a molehill': 'Since she said she couldn't go out with me that evening it's pointless ever asking her out again.'

(4) *Minimisation.* Misinterpreting one's achievement so that its actual worth is underestimated: 'She seems to enjoy my company, but that's only because there's nobody else available.'

(5) *Dichotomous reasoning.* Categorising oneself as one thing or the other, as a success or a failure, with no intermediate position: 'She doesn't like me; that's because I'm basically unlikeable.'

(6) *Arbitrary inference.* Making a negative inference from something

---

DAILY RECORD OF THOUGHTS

Date	Situation	Sad Emotion	Thoughts
	Describe:	Rate degree of	Write thoughts that
	(1) Actual event leading to sad emotion.	emotion 1–100.	preceded emotion.
	(2) Stream of thoughts, daydreams or recollection leading to unpleasant emotion.		

Examples

16/2	Thinking of all the things I had to do over the next week.	40	Felt 'I'll never be able to get everything done.'
17/2	Paul phoned to say he can't go out with me tonight because he has to work.	60	'He doesn't like me as much as he used to.'
18/2	Made three mistakes typing one letter.	30	'I'm just not functioning as well as I used to.'

Explanation: When you experience a sad emotion, note the situation that seemed to give rise to the emotion (if the emotion occurred while you were thinking, daydreaming, etc. please note this). Then note the thought associated with the emotion. In rating degree of the emotion 1 = trace and 100 = the most intense possible.

(After Beck *et al.*, 1979.)

Fig. 10.3. Daily record of thoughts.

without taking into account alternative explanations: 'She arrived late which means she didn't really want to come anyway'.

(7) *Selective abstraction.* Basing a conclusion on one fact taken out of context while ignoring any conflicting evidence: 'Although she has kept all our other arrangements the fact that she didn't come tonight means she is not committed to our relationship.'

It can be seen that some thoughts are examples of more than one mechanism in play; indeed, the example above of over-generalisation might also result from personalisation, magnification or selective abstraction.

Basic beliefs

In cognitive therapy the therapist attempts to identify more fundamental assumptions which are held to be the basis of that depressed person's automatic thoughts. Examples of these might be 'Unless I am a success socially I will never by happy' or 'My worth as a person depends on what others think about me.' In a relapse prevention programme, however, the aim is more limited in helping individuals to gain some realisation of how illogical thinking is linked to feelings of depression and what their particular thoughts may be when they feel depressed.

Behavioural approaches

These have linked depression to a decrease in those behaviours which are positively reinforcing or rewarding to the person (Lewinsohn *et al.*, 1982). This might come about as a result of a sudden change in circumstances such as loss of a valued job or the end of a supportive relationship, or because of a more chronically unrewarding environment.

Example
Gill's new job paid well but she did miss the company of all the colleagues she had had in her previous one. Rather than working in a large open-plan office with four other secretaries, she was now in her own office working as the boss's private secretary. With the pay rise she had moved to a new flat but this meant travelling further to meet her friends, and because she was anxious about travelling by public transport in the evenings and weekends she ended up seeing them less often.

Interacting with work colleagues and friends had been a considerable source of pleasure and support for Gill, perhaps more rewarding than she had realised at the time. As a result of her new job and a change of accommodation she now had much less contact with them and life had begun to seem generally less enjoyable.

So not only may depression arise as a result of a decrease in rewarding behaviour, but depressed individuals tend to engage in fewer activities anyway, so that a vicious cycle may develop. Into the bargain those activities that they do participate in they rate as less enjoyable than before.

Example
Gill had actually made two new friends close to her new flat, but as she became more generally despondent she didn't seem to have the same energy or desire to visit them or go out with them. Even when she did get around to going out with them for a meal or to the cinema she didn't seem to enjoy it so much.

Behavioural treatment of depression attempts to increase the potential for positive reward in the individual's life by encouraging activities likely to be pleasant, particularly those that have been enjoyed by the person in the past. This may be attempted by means of graded task assignments while the person keeps a daily record of activities so that the level and quality of activities can be monitored.

Also depressed feelings may lift when alternative sources of reward are found and utilised, but to identify and use these the individual often requires certain skills. The depressed person typically behaves in a passive, reactive way and a degree of assertiveness or other social skills may be required to behave in a manner which evokes rewarding attention and interest from others. If the requisite skills are lacking the person's depression may be perpetuated and may even worsen. The person's skills to capitalise on potentially rewarding situations may be enhanced by means of skills training especially in social skills and assertiveness.

Example
Although Mike wished he could speak a second language better, he had felt very anxious about going on his own to an evening class where he would not know anyone. After rehearsing some aspects of attending a first class in the social skills group, he was able to take the plunge and managed to cope. Mike managed to continue attending

classes and eventually got more friendly with two of the others there, who admitted they had also been apprehensive about attending the first class. He also made good progress with his French!

References

Beck, A. *et al.* (1979) *Cognitive Therapy of Depression.* Wiley, Chichester.

Cummings, C., Gordon, J. and Marlatt, G.A. (1980) 'Relapse: Strategies of prevention and prediction.' In W.R. Miller (Ed) *The Addictive Behaviours.* Pergamon Press, Oxford.

Lewinsohn, P.M., Sullivan, J.M. and Grosscup, S.J. (1982) 'Behavioural therapy: clinical implications.' In A.J. Rush (Ed) *Short Term Psychotherapies for Depression.* Wiley, Chichester.

Marlatt, G.A. and Gordon, J.R. (Eds) (1985) *Relapse Prevention.* Guilford Press, London.

Chapter 11

Putting It All Together

This chapter describes ways in which relapse prevention techniques could be integrated in the final phase of the programme. For the clients, the application of the coping skills learnt in the programme has to be made under stressful real-life conditions. The decisions that have to be made are 'hot decisions' without the comfort of the group and the presence of the therapist.

This chapter looks at ways of recreating 'as live as possible' situations within the framework of a group or session. A typical timetable is given in Fig. 11.1. We describe our explorations into producing trance-like states to create a psychological state similar to pre-relapse states. Our approach is also aimed at increasing the client's self-efficacy by practising 'coping' in such situations.

Creating the world in the group

Overton (1972) showed that things learnt when intoxicated are better recalled in an intoxicated state than in a normal state. This effect is called *state-dependent learning*. This could mean that the coping skills learnt during the programme have been learnt in a 'normal state' and may have to be applied in different psychological states (when a person is under pressure, when the person has had a lapse, etc.). Clients may have already pointed out role-playing set situations is very different from coping in real life. The problem of translating skills learnt using techniques such as role play in group situations can be partly attributed to state-dependent learning.

It has been shown (Lowe, 1987) that when people are asked to imagine that they are drunk they show cognitive and behavioural deficits as though actually drunk. This indicates that states associated with relapse can be accessed by techniques such as imagery, guided fantasy and trance inducement.

We have found it a very powerful and effective strategy to integrate the skills and techniques of the programme by getting the clients to select the appropriate coping skills in induced pre-relapse states. Cue exposure (see Chapter 1) is another technique that can be used to create pre-relapse states in the client within a group session.

Taking the group into the world

Another way of increasing the 'as live as possible' element in the programme is to literally take the group out into the world. Situations that are encountered using real life are much less predictable and much more complicated and necessitate clients to think on their feet a little more. They would be put in a position of having to select coping techniques from the relapse prevention menu. This is also useful when teaching skills such as social skills, assertion and refusal of the addictive substance. Some ways of doing this are highlighted in Chapter 12.

Relapse prevention paraphernalia

Throughout the relapse prevention programme we have advocated the carrying of cue cards, reminder cards, balance sheets, diaries, etc. Many of these are for use in pre-relapse states, when clients find it difficult to think straight. In scenes that are set up in this stage of the programme, clients should be encouraged to use all the relapse prevention paraphernalia.

Notes for therapists

Exercise 1

The aim of this exercise is to recreate the 'sense' and the 'feel' of a pre-relapse state and then engineer situations in which the client has to use his or her new-found coping strategies.

The situation should be as practical as possible. At the same time therapists should be cautious that they set up situations that can be contained. It is essential that the clients are sufficiently debriefed at the end of the session (e.g. with relaxation exercises and positive suggestions).

It is difficult to time these exercises. They may take 10 minutes or

SESSION TIMETABLE

PUTTING IT ALL TOGETHER

Aims of the session

- To access pre-lapse/relapse emotional states.
- To help utilise skills/strategies learnt during the programme in such an emotional state.
- To reiterate and reinforce course content.
- To increase client self-efficacy by the reference experience of coping with such an emotional state.
- To elicit feedback from the client about the programme.

Time (minutes)	Objective	Content/activity
10	Feedback from previous session	
10	Eliciting of members' feelings about the 'last session'	Group leader mentioning that this is the last group; ask about their feelings.
10	Discussion on importance of putting it all together	Talk on state-dependent learning.
	Introduce objectives of the session (see above)	
10	Explain exercise	Brief talk on accessing emotional state (danger zones) and using skills learnt during the programme, making decision in those states.
15	Carry out exercise	Pick a volunteer and ask him or her to sit comfortably and close their eyes. Then give instructions of the selected exercise (use Exercise 1 or Exercise 2).

Fig. 11.1. Session timetable: putting it all together.

Time (minutes)	Objective	Content/activity
		Note – be conscious of debriefing and add positive suggestions at the end.
	Repeat with other volunteers	
10	Coffee break	
10	Feedback	
15	Recap of course	Talk by the therapist about all aspects of the course.
	Verbal feedback	
10	Form filling Follow-up arrangements Relaxation exercise	

Fig. 11.1. Session timetable: putting it all together continued

longer. The exercise needs to be done one person at a time. In a group a different situation should be used for each person if possible. Those observing should gain as much from the exercise, by association and empathy, as the individual doing it.

We have used two types of *situations* and different *levels of help* for the client in this exercise. These are outlined below.

Situation types
(1) *Immediate confrontation.* This is like exposure to drug, substance, equipment, etc. (see cue exposure Chapter 1) or imagined exposure.
(2) *Problematic situation.* Here the client is presented with problems to solve. This could be a typical or personal high-risk situation.

Levels of help
(1) The coping responses which have already been worked out are written up on the board.
(2) Every one in the group brainstorms coping strategies which are written up on the board before the role-play.
(3) As above, but the coping strategies are not written up on the board, so there is no permanent reminder.
(4) Broad triggers are written up on a board as reminders: 'what

thoughts should you have?', 'what should you say to yourself?', 'what should you do?', 'what problem-solving technique should you use?', etc.

(5) No help at all.

The client who volunteers is asked to sit comfortably slightly apart from the rest of the group members. He or she is then asked to recreate the situation which has been worked out before (eyes closed if it helps). They are asked to do this by talking aloud as they build up the image or situation mentally. It is important that they repeat their thoughts aloud throughout the exercise. Once the situation has been created the therapist should prompt the client to follow his or her own initiative and should withdraw as much as possible.

The exercise should always be engineered to end in the successful use of coping strategies. It may be necessary at times to increase the level of help during the exercise, but obviously the therapist should cope with his or her own anxiety and allow the client space.

Some examples of situations

- Replaying a recently experienced high risk situation or lapse.
- Presenting the client with the object of their addiction – a drink, a large cream cake, a small amount of white powder wrapped in foil, etc. – or an imagined visit to a pub, bookmaker, casino, etc.
- *Scenario*: A very busy day with little time to think. Although you had began the day energetically, your poor sleep due to the hot night is beginning to sap your energy. It took half an hour to get home from work, the journey had little of interest and passed by mechanically. As you arrive home the house is bursting with energy, it feels as though half the children in the street are running in and out shouting. You usually either prepare the evening meal or look after the children. You don't get much of a welcome greeting, in fact it's more of a catalogue of instructions and orders...
- *Scenario*: You live in a grotty bedsit, with worn out fifties furniture. It's midday and you have just crawled out from the covers, put on the radio and made a strong cup of coffee. You've got nothing planned for the day and stare into space. After a short while there is a loud shout and a simultaneous knock at the front door. Pete and Debbie are standing there, grinning and obviously not straight. They spread into the bedsit, keeping up a continuous patter as they sit down and exclaim 'Look what we've got!' ...

Warning!

It is important to diffuse group members' feelings after the exercise, as many of the group members will have identified with the situation and be experiencing quite strong cravings. It is often the case that they don't tell this to the group leader. Everyone should be encouraged to use their coping techniques to lower the emotional tone and reduce tension. You may need to finish the exercise with more than one client if others become involved. Always do a different exercise (a fun game or relaxation exercise) after this to minimise the risk of somebody walking out still experiencing the pre-lapse state.

Sometimes you may find that other exercises in the programme trigger individuals into similar emotional states. If this happens, it is important to change the tack of the group and follow through with the individual, trying out coping strategies until he or she has successfully worked through the feelings. When this happens naturally within the course of a group it provides a very powerful modelling experience. It becomes an excellent demonstration of the efficacy of relapse prevention techniques.

Exercise 2

This exercise is similar to the previous one and is closely linked to 'descriptions of past relapses' and 'relapse fantasies' described in Chapter 1. The same rules of help and debriefing as in Exercise 1 apply to this exercise.

Get the volunteer to sit comfortably, close his or her eyes and imagine a situation when they have had a 'slip'. If appropriate they can recreate mentally the last occasion when they had a lapse or relapse. When the person has got 'into the situation' the therapist asks them to describe the 'thoughts' and 'feelings' they are having. When the person has gained sufficient 'access' to the 'relapse state' (observe changes in physiology such as breathing, posture, etc.) they are then asked to cope with the feelings and thoughts using the skills and techniques available to them. Help is given to the individual as required and the rest of the group are also encouraged to offer help and suggestions.

Again the experience is engineered to end on a positive note with the use of skills and techniques in the relapse prevention menu. Use same caution regarding debriefing, as outlined in the previous exercise.

References

Lowe, G. (1987) 'Imagined states of sobriety – effects on alcohol-induced behavioural deficits.' Paper presented at the British Psychological Society Annual Conference.

Overton, D.A. (1972) 'State-dependent learning produced by alcohol and its relevance to alcoholism.' In B. Kissin and H. Begleiter (Eds) *Physiology and behavior. The biology of alcoholism, vol 2.* Plenum, New York.

Chapter 12

Troubleshooting

This chapter is designed to be of help when problems arise. We have outlined some of the problems that happened to us during the course of running groups or with individuals, and we have made some suggestions about how to cope with the situation. Many of the problems that are likely to arise are a consequence of normal group processes or relate to the normal everyday difficulties in dealing with people, and we will not discuss these. We anticipate that group leaders will use their knowledge and experience to work with these situations. There will of course be 'one-offs' that no one can anticipate. In the group of long-term heroin users which we ran, one of the members produced a gun in the middle off a session and only after a very long five minutes did we discover that it was a starting pistol!

Some of the problems that may arise relate to particular attitudes, beliefs or ideas that some group members have had and that have proved difficult to shift. It is impossible to include all such problems but we hope to give you a flavour of them.

This chapter is not intended to be read as a whole but dipped into when issues occur or skimmed through as a preparation for the rough and tumble of running a group. The addictions that each problem most relates to have been highlighted.

Lack of awareness of thought processes

All addictions

Everybody has the problem that they are not aware of their own internal conversation all the time. Indeed if we were it would cause a great deal of problems. However, some people are more keenly in tune with the thoughts that run through their minds than others. We believe, in line with cognitive theories, that thoughts precede action, thus making the content of the thoughts extremely important. An under-standing and awareness of thoughts leading up to a relapse situation is essential with the relapse prevention model. Many of the exercises in the groups require the group members to record thoughts/images. If a client is one of the many people who have difficulty in this area he or she is at risk of getting very little from the group programme.

Clients will often say that something 'just happened' and they had no idea how a situation or mood came about. However, the exercises and homework tasks will obviously help in the process of increasing self awareness. Sometimes clients need some extra help with this. This is best given as early in the programme as possible. Here are some suggestions to increase a client's awareness of his or her thought processes:

• *'Now' game.*   Somebody in the group shouts out 'Now!' every few minutes and as they do so everyone has to say the last thought that went through their mind, using the exact words. This could be written down. This can be played at home by asking someone else to shout 'Now!' or by using a watch which bleeps at regular intervals instead.

• *Free association.*   This is best done in a one-to-one situation. Simply ask the client to say aloud anything that comes into his or her mind, as it happens. The client can use a form of verbal shorthand, if necessary, and any cognition which would take too long to explain can be re-viewed at the end.

• Try to recreate risky situations, as in the putting it all together session (see Chapter 11). As the situation is unravelled the client has to speak all his or her thoughts aloud. In this way chains of dangerous thoughts may be identified.

Clients who continually find obstacles and problems

All addictions

Anyone who has ever dealt with people will recognise this. Frequently it is seen when clients do not do homework tasks, make it difficult to set homework or do not seem to be able to adjust the way some things are done – for example, a very sexually promiscuous woman who cannot dress less provocatively because she does not feel dressed rightly any other way. When this pattern appears to be emerging the information needs to be fed back to the client tactfully. If this does not produce any change in behaviour or the ensuing conversation is not fruitful, it is useful to go back to the balance sheet and review the client's current position. Often the balance has changed during the course. Sometimes reviewing the balance sheet at a later stage highlights the elements that have always been there but are more important to the individual than was originally supposed.

The intention in using the balance sheet is to reframe the therapeutic problem, away from seeing the client as being awkward, difficult, etc., into an expression of their ambivalence about changing their addictive pattern. The balance sheet lays out what the ambivalence consists of and is therefore 'recognising' the problem for the individual. This allows them to remake the decision about continuing their addiction or not. It also prevents them from easing their dissonance (psychological tension resulting from inconsistent or incompatible ideas or behaviour, such as in a nearly equally balanced balance sheet) by finding problems in the world around them.

Excessive self-criticism

All addictions

This is a characteristic of many people who have psychological problems, but we have decided to mention it here because it is so often a striking feature with people who have addiction problems. Failure and guilt seem to prevail in the field of addictions. Self-criticism lies at the heart of a sense of failure and guilt, often bringing with it depression and low self-esteem. Cummings, Gordon and Marlatt (1980) found that negative emotional states with intrapersonal origin are the most likely reported cause of relapse across a range of addictions, and a cognitive style with strong self criticism is very likely to precipitate such a state. If this is very pronounced we suggest that the group leaders should consult more general work on cognitive therapy and on cognitive therapy for depression. However, we have outlined a few ideas which might help.

• Whenever an example arises ask the client to explain briefly to the rest of the group the circumstances and the thoughts they had about themselves. Then ask everyone in turn to say briefly whether they thought the client's assessment of themselves was reasonable or not. This allows clients to have realistic feedback about themselves.

• Try to find out if the self-criticism relates to particular themes, such as having bad relationships or disappointing others, etc. Once you have a theme ask the client to describe the opposite sides to the theme, e.g. good and bad relationships. Then ask the client which of these they would prefer to be described as. After they have chosen ask the client 'What are the advantages of the chosen side as you see it in contrast to the disadvantages of the other side?' As they do this they will have described an idea which is more central and fundamental to their way of understanding or looking at the world.

When they have given you the advantages and disadvantages ask them to again choose which of these they would prefer to be described as, and then to explain the advantages and disadvantages of this. This process is repeated until the client is unable or unwilling to continue. Depending on the original idea it may take two steps or ten steps before the sequence comes to a halt.

This process is called laddering, and was described by Hinkle (1965). It is frequently used in personal construct therapy, in order to learn more about how an idea fits into a person's view of the world.

If this approach is not useful it is possible to follow a similar process in reverse. This is similar to that described by Landfield (1971). Instead of asking for the advantages and disadvantages, the group leader asks 'How do you know that . . .' In this way the idea or theme becomes more and more concrete and is laddered down.

'People who aren't like me (drinker, user, etc.) are boring'

Drugs, alcohol and smoking

This is an idea we have heard frequently, especially among drug users and young people with alcohol problems. It relates to an attitude about the image of the use of a substance. We have come across a similar notion in 'stop smoking' groups. Usually it is an entrenched image which weighs heavily on the 'I want to continue' side of the balance sheet.

This attitude/image provides the kind of tantalisation that reasserts itself prior to relapse, and is therefore a very dangerous concept for a would-be abstinent person to hold. The idea is usually boosted by memories of good times when things were more under control. The concept will be linked to other ideas around this theme; the two that we have encountered are a fear of losing social skills, and becoming 'boring' themselves and being perceived by others as boring. These ideas can be embedded into their self-image, so that loss of the concept/image involves a painful change in identity – from being a radical protestor against society or a sociable chatty person to being a bore who is the same as everyone else.

We have found that it is important to begin by exploring with the person exactly what they mean by a 'bore' and what is its opposite (what they wish to be). Try to then get the client to describe the behaviour of a bore and its opposite. (How do you know someone is a bore? What do they do or not do, exactly?) Once you have obtained the two descriptions, set up a field experiment by asking the client to observe sets of people and test out whether the groups actually fit into his or her concept of what he or she wishes to be. Usually they don't. The client also needs to identify other groups that fit into the 'what I want to be like' image. It is important to make this a practical experiment for the client as we have found that this is a much more potent method of change than analysing and rationalising the concept alone.

Inconsistent attendance and dropouts

All addictions

Anybody who works in the addiction field will be used to this problem and will no doubt already have their own methods of dealing with the situation as it arises. However, this is a suggestion to those who are new to the field.

If several people in the group are failing to attend it is important first to assess the atmosphere and culture of the group. We assume that therapists will use their group skills to resolve or work with this situation by, for example, bringing the non-attendance up as an item in the group, considering how much space individuals have to talk, what interpersonal dynamics might be contributing to the situation, whether other things are happening outside the group setting, etc.

When one or two people are attending inconsistently or have dropped out it is useful to assume that the decision to continue/not to continue their addictive behaviour has changed, and hence they may have decided to move back into the contemplation or non-action phase (Prochaska and Di Clementi's model). If someone has dropped out and they cannot be enticed back into the group it is useful to offer them an individual appointment. If neither of these is possible send them details of this exercise and ask them to go through it themselves.

Quite often there has not been a positive, conscious decision to go back to their addictive behaviour or to give up therapy, but their behaviour shows an ambivalence in the decision. It is the job of the group leader to help examine the pros and cons for the client so that the decision is acknowledged and conscious. This is done by asking the client to work through a balance sheet. If the client works through the balance sheet and reaches the conclusion that he or she does not want to change their behaviour then they will obviously leave the group. Try not to let the other group members persuade the client with emotionally laden arguments, but to respect his or her decision.

However, the balance of factors has often changed for identifiable reasons, and some of these can be addressed. Here are some examples:

• Fatigue and tiredness. It is hard work trying to change entrenched behaviours. Maybe a break is needed, not from trying to change but from high-risk situations, so arrange a visit to a haunt where you can't use, a course of Antabuse, a visit to a health farm, etc.

• Lost sight of goals. The gains of stopping have receded into the distance and have lost their clarity. (See 'balance sheet' section later in this chapter.)

• Other factors have either emerged or are more important than originally thought. These would have to be dealt with individually.

• Practical problems may have evolved such as child care which it is possible to resolve, or housing which is much less easy and may necessitate other agencies becoming involved.

Lapses and relapses during therapy

All addictions

During a relapse prevention course it is inevitable that this will happen to some of the members. Although this is obviously not a desirable outcome it can provide a very useful learning experience for the client and the group. An atmosphere needs to be created which encourages people to attend when they have relapsed. Often clients miss a week or two and then return. A rule for the client to contact every week even if they do not attend is extremely useful.

When a client next attends after a lapse has occurred it is important to put off the business of the group and take some time to look at the relapse in detail. In order to do this ask the client to retell the story of the lapse in detail. When he or she has done this encourage the group and the client to look for triggers, high-risk situations and seemingly irrelevant decisions leading up to the lapse. Once these have been identified brainstorm ways in which it could have been handled differently, including looking at coping skills in situations leading up to the lapse.

Conflict with 'Anonymous addicts'

Alcohol, drugs and gambling

The Anonymous organisations have helped thousands of people to stop their addictive behaviour. Up until recent years, they have been the only source of help for a great many people, and still are the only source in some areas. Alcoholics Anonymous, Narcotics Anonymous and Gamblers Anonymous all hold a medical model of addiction problems. The medical model suggests that some people are born with a predisposition to be an alcoholic, drug user, etc., it is therefore no fault of the person with an addiction that they are ill (addicted). The Anonymous model also suggests that the only form or treatment is total abstinence. This model is currently very prevalent in the addictions field in America. The relapse prevention model and the Anonymous model are fundamentally different in their understanding of addictions. It is not uncommon for clients to attend Anonymous meetings whilst also receiving help from statutory and voluntary agencies. It can become extremely confusing for people to have two different philosophies presented at the same time.

It is essential for the worker to find ways of working together with the Anonymous organisations, as they are essential components in the support of so many clients. A conflict may occur with some people who attend Anonymous meetings, if they hold the medical (disease) model belief strongly. The potential areas of conflict with the relapse prevention work, that we have experienced are: the psychosocial model, techniques of countering lapses and relapses, rule violation effect and controlled use.

Do not try to convert clients to a psychological model of their addiction, but find common denominators on which to work. All the techniques aimed at reducing the chances of a slip are compatible between the theories, such as self monitoring, building up coping strategies, lifestyle balance, analysis of high-risk situations and triggers, etc. A client who follows the disease model will only choose to differ at certain reasonably predictable times. (Spot the eyes glaze over!) As the therapeutic goal for each client is discussed individually this will have little impact on the group unless the client is intolerant of others. Although the theoretical model is important to provide a cohesive frame to treatment, it is not essential, as long as the client can productively utilise the pot pourri of copying strategies on offer. This means that the rule violation effect and strategies for coping with a relapse provide the greatest difficulty within the groups, but as these are only a small proportion of the whole package, clients who hold these beliefs can still gain a great deal from the sessions. In our experience negotiation about common aims is the best way forward, taking care to respect the clients' beliefs.

For us, one of the delights of working within the relapse prevention framework has been, that we have understood and appreciated why the Anonymous organisations work so well. In particular its ability to enable lifestyle changes to be made, by providing alternative non-addictive social activities and friends to share this with. The belief system adopted is a kind of cognitive reframing (albeit with some dangers) and the other members of the fellowship provide role models who encourage the possibility that 'I can do it to!'

Balance sheet

All addictions

When a client completes a balance sheet the positive pay offs from stopping the addictive behaviour are often very vague and a long time in the future. This is especially true of addictive behaviours which have a detrimental effect on health. Feeling more 'with it' or healthier are very difficult things to assess and they do not happen suddenly. They are the result of a gradual change. The same is true of resolving a chaotic lifestyle or a financial mess.

When a balance sheet assessment is done at the beginning of the process of trying to change the positive pay offs usually seem very distant and intangible for the client. This means that they are unlikely to be very motivated by the prospect of them. As a group leader it is important to sharpen up the positive pay offs to make maximum use and give maximum help to the client. This can be done in a number of ways:

● Specify and clarify as much as possible what the pay offs might be. For example 'healthy' might be not being breathless going up the stairs or having more energy, 'less chaotic' might be having three planned events in the week which the client attends.

● Find out from other people who have successfully changed their behaviour what was different for them, and when they noticed the difference.

● Set a timescale for looking at the improvements and a method for doing so. You may be able to use some assessment tools for this (Beck depression scale, liver function blood test, carbonmonoxide in breath). More probably you will have to invent something for yourself such as a simple 1–10 scale on 'how good I feel when I get up in the morning' for three days every fourth week. If you do use any formal measure or descriptive record it is important for the client to assess him or herself at the beginning of the process so that you can compare results.

'Thoughts all over the place'

All addictions

Every therapist will have come across clients whose thought processes seem to be totally associational and who appear not to have cohesive strings of ideas. Typically it is very difficult to piece together information about the client, although they will often have been verbose.

In the language of personal construct theory they have a loose construct system. In other words there appears to be little structure or logic to their thoughts. This is often exacerbated by anxiety, which tends to increase the ruminative and associational nature of thoughts. An example of this is a lady who was terribly anxious following what she saw as a disastrous trip to the shops. When she told her tale, which took 30 minutes to unfold and be understood by the therapist, she confused and blurred other incidents which had gone wrong on other occasions, oscillating between her personal history, her feelings and thoughts at the time, the actual incident (which was very vaguely told), fatalistic suppositions about the future and general remarks about the world. Needless to say it took a great deal of effort to unravel the facts of the incident, let alone her thoughts. Clearly a client like this can be very difficult to deal with and progress with. It may not always be prudent to include these clients in a group format.

From the description of the problem it is clear that working with clients who have this kind of cognitive structure can be very time consuming. As long as there is no other reason for this kind of cognitive structure/processing – for example brain damage following overdoses or excessive alcohol consumption – then there are two rules to adopt when attempting to work with clients:

● *Relaxation.* Spend a great deal of time working on methods of relaxation and lifestyle modification as increases in anxiety greatly exacerbate the problem.

- *Structure.*   Structure everything! Make the content of the sessions topic lead rather than event lead. Keep refocusing on the topic when the session strays. Write the facts and logic down on paper or a white board so that it is easier to distil the issues from other things. Stick to facts as much as possible: it helps to increase the proportion of direct rather than open questions. Try to make inroads into circular and trapped thinking by writing this down and going through each stage of the thought process looking at the logic of it and the evidence. This style needs to be continued ad nauseam. It is very hard work for the therapist, who often gets frustrated. It is easy for this frustration to be redirected into the need for structure for the client; when this happens the need to impose structure can easily slip over to a non-empathetic, assertive counselling style which is non-productive.

Blind determination

Overeating, alcohol and smoking

We would expect most therapists to recognise this attitude/behaviour. It is not an uncommon occurrence to come across someone who very much wants to change their addictive behaviour but feels that if they simply try hard enough it will happen. We have seen attention slip away when we have discussed predicting high-risk situations because 'it won't happen to me' or 'I just know I can't drink any more'.

This is an attitude about the way of changing addictive behaviours that we have come across in several addictive fields, particularly over-eating, alcohol and smoking. It may be that this belief is prevalent in these areas because many people have managed to change their behaviour in relation to these without help, and a mythology to the effect that 'motivation equals success' has built up. The essence of the belief is that if you try hard enough you will be able to resist temptation.

This attitude leads to people not believing a slip or relapse will happen to them '... because I really want to stop'. Unfortunately, this can lead to their not taking note of how to escape from a craving situation or how to stop a slip turning into a relapse. The idea of effort alone as the route to success often leads to the testing out of personal control: 'If I can cope with this I must be alright now'. Clearly it is a dangerous concept because it is likely to precipitate a relapse and clients take less from the package of relapse prevention ideas to help them control their behaviour.

This concept usually derives from a more important, higher order belief or construct such as a reluctance to seek help; acceptance and particular interpretation of the 'Anonymous' model; or a very matter-of-fact, concrete, unpsychological model of the world. The idea should be explored so that the group leader understands the client's individual connotations. We have outlined some approaches that we have taken with some of the ways this idea has been expressed:

● *Failure too painful.* Blind determination can be driven by the fear of failure or the very real high cost of failure, such as marital break-up. To ameliorate this review the notion of one slip not equalling failure but being a learning experience, and short-term versus long-term goals. It may also be possible to undertake some contracting with significant others to relieve some of the pressure.

● *Unpsychological model of the world.* If the blind determination is a consequence of a very concrete, unpsychological model of the world it is best not to tackle the blind determination directly but to hope that the client will absorb other psychological ideas from the course. If this is the case the client will only take a limited amount from the relapse prevention package, but this can be helpful to them and sometimes is enough to control their addiction.

● *Conflict with 'Anonymous' model.* See section earlier in this chapter.

● *Reluctance to seek help.* Often people who come for help with addictions are people who would not habitually seek help, but the addiction or circumstances arising from it have lead to their having to seek help. Although such individuals are committed to changing, the process of being in treatment is difficult for them. One such person described it as feeling stupid after every session. He reacted to this feeling/thought by giving the content of the sessions little thought outside of the sessions themselves and increasing his personal effort. If this is the construct at the root of a client's blind determination the group leader should examine with the client the concept of what it means to seek help and change the approach to be more client lead: the client devises all the homework assignments, the educator role is emphasised, etc.

Controlling anger

All addictions

The precipitants of the majority of relapses concern unpleasant feelings (Cummings, Gordon and Marlatt, 1980) such as depression and anger. We do not usually run a group session specifically about anger, but this may be indicated by the composition of the group or an additional session may be needed for some of the members. Many of the ideas in the relapse prevention model apply to current techniques of anger control, for example identifying precipitant and high-risk situations. In situations themselves, using relaxation and coping self-statements are used as well as working on voice tone and body language. We also feel that working on lifestyle balance has a preventative role in dealing with anger control. However, if anger control is an issue for your client we suggest that you read *Clinical Approaches to Aggression and Violence* by Kevin Howells and Clive Hollin, published by the British Psychological Society.

Role-plays not translating to the real world

All addictions

Group treatments are often criticised because they appear as false, and sometimes they do not have much effect when dealing with real people in the real world. This can happen with any role-play – high-risk situations, assertion, using self-control strategies, etc. If you find that doing role-plays seems to be having little effect on the way clients are coping in real situations we suggest three ways of increasing the impact of the roleplays:

(1) 'Move 'em out!' In other words take the role-play out from the group setting into the real world: drink refusal in a pub is much more powerful than in a group. Use people 'not in the know' such as a shopkeeper who sells the 'desired item': buy something else instead from the shop.

(2) Make the group settings more real by inviting in friends or relatives for a role-play, or by the group going out and observing a difficult situation, then role-playing it as they saw it. This adds lots of the little extras that happen in everyday life into the group. It makes the situations a little less predictable and more complicated, and relies on the individuals in the role-play to think on their feet a little more.

(3) Sometimes a role-play lacks credence because the risk or stakes are not present to increase the pressure, as they would be in the real situation. This can be resolved by adding in other pressures or costs to the role-play situation, such as a financial penalty with the money going to the client's least favourite charity, a commitment to do jobs for other group members or to begin an exercise regime which is supervised/observed by a group member or leader.

Self-efficacy

All addictions

Two frequent characteristics of people coming for help to maintain control of their addictive behaviour is that they don't really know where to start and so feel helpless, or they have an idea of what to do but don't feel capable of doing it. Self-efficacy is the term we use in connection with the latter. It is the client's assessment of his or her ability to do a task successfully. Whether this is positive or negative obviously has a great bearing on whether the client will tackle a situation or task and the probable outcome.

It has been shown that belief about the outcome of something affects that outcome dramatically: this is called the self-fulfilling prophecy (Festinger, 1964). Most people have realistic beliefs about their ability to do some things and not others. However, a large number of people underestimate their skills or have learned to be pessimistic about their ability to control their addiction because of past failures. A client with a pessimistic view of their ability to do homework tasks or cope in situations is likely not to do very well and may put up blocks all the time.

If you have a client who has low self-efficacy it is important to try to alter this view of him or herself. This is best done experientially through the successful completion of tasks. Maximising self-efficacy is important for everybody who is trying to change their behaviour. Self-efficacy can be monitored for drinkers by using the Situational Confidence Questionnaire – 39 (Annis, 1984). Workers in other fields might find it useful to look at this and attempt an ad hoc adaptation for their client group (see Chapter 4). Maximising self-efficacy is done by making sure that:

- Any assignments or tasks are perceived as challenging – in the past they resulted in drinking/using or some other form of 'not coping'.

- The task is seen as directly related to the process of controlling the addiction.

- Only a moderate amount of effort was needed to cope effectively.

- Few external aids were used to cope successfully, so that the client attributes success to him or herself rather than to a partner, a drug, the therapist, etc.

- The task is part of an overall pattern of success, so that a steady improvement is seen.

• There is minimum use of avoidance strategies as a method of coping.

All of these points are aimed at increasing the likelihood that clients will attribute success to their own ability to cope and increase personal control. It may be necessary to review the attributing process if the client still does not take the praise for success. This can be done by externalising the thought processes: ask the client to tell the group how he or she thinks about the event or situation that has happened, write this down on a flipchart and ask for views from the group.

Beware! Sessions causing relapse

Drugs and smoking

We have seen this happen in 'stop smoking' groups and groups for controlling heroin use. However this could potentially happen in any addictive field. What happened was simply that the relapse prevention session appeared to trigger a craving for some people and they walked out from the group to their dealers or the tobacconist. The very explicit conversation about high-risk situations, routines of use, etc., created a craving or urge with a rise in arousal. This tended to happen early on in the group course before we had taught urge control techniques, and often wasn't mentioned for a couple of weeks.

We feel that this is most likely to happen to clients who are ambivalent about giving up and those who are not used to talking about the mechanics of giving up. It is unlikely to happen to clients who attend Anonymous group meetings because they will have been exposed to detailed conversation before.

Prevention seems to be better than cure for this problem. We therefore introduced a signal system (e.g. waving a hand) for clients to indicate if they were getting 'wound up' by the topic of conversation in the group. If a client was affected we would break the topic and do a brief relaxation exercise. Obviously we would then check out with the client later in the group.

We found that the timing of the group was important. If it was part of a day programme it was better placed in the middle or at the beginning of the day. Alternatively a low-key activity should follow it. If the group was the clients' only treatment we always ended the group with the relaxation exercises and left the room for them to sit and drink tea or coffee in for the next hour to allow them some time to distract themselves and plan how they would deal with the next few hours.

One of the most important elements was to raise the problem as a potential danger so that clients could then raise it more easily. It is important not to present it as a very serious problem as this can be self-fulfilling and discourage explicit conversation about the use of the addictive substance.

Managing controlled and abstinent clients in the same group

Drugs, alcohol, risky sexual behaviour

Philosophically, there should be no problem in mixing members of a group who have different overall aims. However as we all know in practice things are rarely so easy. Much of the course will apply equally to people who are aiming to be abstinent and those who are aiming to control their addiction, for example identifying high-risk situations, self-control strategies, lifestyle balance, etc., but clients who aim to control their behaviour will also need additional self-control strategies such as arriving late to allow less drinking time, taking a limited amount of money out with them, monitoring blood alcohol levels, etc. You may wish to include these 'extras' in the mainstream of a group or to have an additional session. This will obviously depend on the composition of the group.

When clients with these conflicting aims are mixed it is important never to have one isolated person with a different aim. We have found that 25% of the group with the alternative aim is about the smallest proportion that is viable.

Issues that might arise from this mix tend to be to do with splits arising within the group or with an individual's interpretation of his or her aims in relation to the other aims: controlled use may be seen as in some way superior to abstinence, which is for people who are 'too far down the road', or there may be a pressure to persuade abstinent people to 'stop pretending and recognise their problems'.

● *Splits within the group.* Obviously if this arises the group leader should draw upon his or her group skills. Some ideas that may be useful are to do small team work exercises with groups from opposite camps, to choose exercises where the clients need to empathise with the problems of the opposite camp, or to pair abstinent and control clients in a buddy-type system for some tasks.

Occasionally the splits might have a positive spin off. In a group we ran with adolescents one sub-group conformed to the group aims and the other didn't. The social pressure on the 'conform' group was such that it 'dragged' others along with it who might not otherwise have succeeded. In this case if the split had been discouraged it would have been to the detriment of some group members. This was with a naturally occurring group where the social norms and leadership were already established. The process was most probably heightened as the group members were all adolescents.

● *Individual interpretations.*   Some clients may try to demean the other goal or may try to persuade others into their camp. Either of these would suggest some unhappiness, tentativeness or lack of confidence with the decision that the client has come to.

In a very early group that we ran a client who had a controlled drinking aim used to take great relish in telling the other members about his ventures in a pub and embellished his ability to control in a way that was designed to annoy other group members and heighten their craving. One way we found to deal with this was to review their balance sheet on their treatment goal, paying particular attention to the image and connotation that the goal had for them. Sometimes the treatment goal is related to maintaining self-esteem when other things are collapsing or with someone who does not like to ask for help. If this is the case it is important to boost self-esteem by enhancing other areas of competence in a way that is not divisive.

References

Annis, H.M. (1984) *Situational Confidence Questionnaire, Short Form.* Addiction Research Foundation, Toronto.

Cummings, C., Gordon, J. and Marlatt, G.A. (1980) 'Skills training with alcoholics.' *Journal of consulting and Clinical Psychology,* **48**, 305–316.

Festinger, L. (1964) *Conflict, decision and dissonance.* Stanford University Press, Stanford.

Hinkle D. (1965) 'The Change of Personal Constructs from the Viewpoint of a Theory of Construct Implications'. Unpublished PhD Thesis, Ohio State University.

Landfield A.W. (1971) *Personal Construct systems in Psychotherapy.* Rand McNally, Chicago.

(I)

An example of a drink diary. This could be used as an example to devise similar self-monitoring forms for other addictions.

MY DRINK DIARY

Day	Time of drinking	Number of units/pints singles/ glasses of wine etc.*	Type of alcohol	In company or alone	Where drinking took place	Feelings before and afterwards	Effects of drinking	Money spent on alcohol
Mon								
Tue								
Wed								
Thu								
Fri								
Sat								
Sun								
Total units							Total cost	£

* half-pint ordinary beer
  single measure vermouth
1 UNIT = single measure spirits
  1 glass of wine
  1 small glass sherry

1+ UNITS = 1 standard canned lager
2+ UNITS = 1 strong canned lager
4 UNITS = 1 extra strong canned lager

Name: ....

Date of completion: /   /

Appendix A

(II)

Examples of craving diaries, a very useful self-monitoring instrument, especially for abstinence orientated clients and clients with excessive appetites.

CRAVING DIARY 1

Situation	Thoughts/feelings	Belief 0–100%	Other interpretations	Belief 0–100%

CRAVING DIARY 2

Name . . . .

Day/date	Place	Time/who with	Describe how you felt before, during and after craving	What did you do?
Sunday				
Monday				
Tuesday				
Wednesday				
Thursday				
Friday				
Saturday				

Appendix A

(III)

Examples of a questionnaire to evaluate an individual group or a session. This is an adaptation from Session Evaluation Questionnaire (SEQ), Stiles (1980) and credibility of therapy scale, Borkovec and Nau (1972).

References

Borkovec, T.D. and Nau, S.D. (1972) 'Credibility of analogue therapy rationales.' *Journal of Behaviour Therapy and Experimental Psychiatry*, **3**, pp. 252–60.

Stiles, W.B. (1980) 'Measurement of impact of psychotherapy sessions.' *Journal of Consulting and Clinical Psychology*, **48**, pp. 176–85.

SESSION EVALUATION QUESTIONNAIRE

Please circle the number on each line to show how you feel about the session you just had.

This session was:

BAD	1	2	3	4	5	6	7	GOOD
SAFE	1	2	3	4	5	6	7	DANGEROUS
DIFFICULT	1	2	3	4	5	6	7	EASY
VALUABLE	1	2	3	4	5	6	7	WORTHLESS
SHALLOW	1	2	3	4	5	6	7	DEEP
RELAXED	1	2	3	4	5	6	7	TENSE
UNPLEASANT	1	2	3	4	5	6	7	PLEASANT
FULL	1	2	3	4	5	6	7	EMPTY
WEAK	1	2	3	4	5	6	7	POWERFUL
SPECIAL	1	2	3	4	5	6	7	ORDINARY
ROUGH	1	2	3	4	5	6	7	SMOOTH
COMFORTABLE	1	2	3	4	5	6	7	UNCOMFORTABLE

How logical does this approach seem to you?
Not at all   1   2   3   4   5   6   7   Very logical

How useful do you think this approach is?
Not at all   1   2   3   4   5   6   7   Very useful

How confident are you that this approach will be successful?
Not at all   1   2   3   4   5   6   7   Very confident

How confident would you be in recommending this approach to a friend with similar problems?

Not at all   1   2   3   4   5   6   7   Very confident
confident

Please write down any comments you have to make about the session in the space provided.
. . . .

Appendix A

(IV)

Examples of a questionnaire that could be used to evaluate a complete relapse prevention course at the end of it, in terms of client satisfaction.

RELAPSE PREVENTION GROUP – EVALUATION QUESTIONNAIRE

Could you please complete the following questionnaire. This will enable us to make improvements for future groups. Thank you.

Please circle the number you feel is closest to your views.

SESSIONS

1. Relaxation/anxiety management

Not useful   1   2   3   4   5   6   7   Very useful

2. High-risk situations

Not useful   1   2   3   4   5   6   7   Very useful

3. Thought processess in relapse

Not useful   1   2   3   4   5   6   7   Very useful

4. Life style imbalance

Not useful   1   2   3   4   5   6   7   Very useful

5. Assertion/drink refusal

Not useful   1   2   3   4   5   6   7   Very useful

6. Problem solving

Not useful   1   2   3   4   5   6   7   Very useful

7. Drinking imagery

Not useful   1   2   3   4   5   6   7   Very useful

THE COURSE OVERALL

Did you find it

8. Difficult	1	2	3	4	5	6	7	Easy
9. Valuable	1	2	3	4	5	6	7	Worthless
10. Relaxed	1	2	3	4	5	6	7	Tense
11. Full	1	2	3	4	5	6	7	Empty
12. Comfortable	1	2	3	4	5	6	7	Uncomfortable

CONTENT

13. Role play and practice

Too little   1   2   3   4   5   6   7   Too much

14. Teaching and information

Too little   1   2   3   4   5   6   7   Too much

15. Use of video

Too little   1   2   3   4   5   6   7   Too much

continued

16. The length of the sessions

Too short   1   2   3   4   5   6   7   Too long

17. The length of the course

Too short   1   2   3   4   5   6   7   Too long

18. Homework tasks

Too little   1   2   3   4   5   6   7   Too much

19. Home work

Too hard   1   2   3   4   5   6   7   Too easy

20. How logical did you find the course?

Not logical   1   2   3   4   5   6   7   Very logical

21. How confident are you of recommending the course to a friend with similar problems?

Not at all confident   1   2   3   4   5   6   7   Very confident

Appendix A

(V)

Assessment of overall level of functioning
(adapted from the addiction severity index, McLellan **et al.,**
1980)

Introduction

We recommend using this as a clinical instrument to assess and rate
the overall level of functioning of a client. We have used this question-
aire as a structured interview. Its aims are to estimate the severity of
client's problems and assess changes in the overall functioning of the
client.

The questions are aimed at obtaining as much relevant information
as possible to enable the therapist to make a reliable rating. Although
we recommend that the questions be used to structure the interview,
therapists should not feel restricted by them. Any question that the
therapist feels relevant and would help in the rating must be asked.

With practice therapists would find that they are able to make
accurate and reliable ratings.

It must be emphasised this adaptation is meant to be for clinical use
and for basic evaluation of therapy. Those wishing to carry out
scientific outcome research are advised to use the original addiction
severity index (ASI), McLellan *et al.* (1980) and the method of com-
posite scoring, McGahan *et al.* (1982). These can be obtained by writing
to: NIDA, WASHINGTON, DC: USA.

Demographic information

Name/ID number . . . .   Date . . . .
D.O.B . . . .   Age . . . .   Sex . . . .

Marital status
(1) single   (2) married/cohabiting   (3) widowed
(4) separated/divorced

Accommodation
(1) owner occupied   (2) rented   (3) hostel   (4) bed & breakfast
(5) squatting   (6) no fixed abode

Living arrangements
(1) lives alone   (2) lives with friend(s)   (3) lives with parents
(4) lives with spouse/co-habitee   (5) lives with spouse and children
(6) lives alone with children   (7) other . . . .

Employment status
(1) full-time   (2) part time   (3) unemployed   (4) retired   (5) student
(6) house person   (7) other . . . .

Education
(1) left school without exams   (2) OLs   (3) ALs   (4) degree
(5) professional   (6) skilled worker   (7) unskilled   (8) other . . . .

PROFILE										
(1) Medical status	1	2	3	4	5	6	7	8	9	10
(2) Employment/support	1	2	3	4	5	6	7	8	9	10
(3) Alcohol/drug use	1	2	3	4	5	6	7	8	9	10
(4) Other addictions	1	2	3	4	5	6	7	8	9	10
(5) Legal problems	1	2	3	4	5	6	7	8	9	10
(6) Family/social relationships	1	2	3	4	5	6	7	8	9	10
(7) Psychological problems	1	2	3	4	5	6	7	8	9	10

Summary of client profile

Medical status

(1) Have you been hospitalised for a medical problem?
   If yes, how many times? . . . . (include detoxes)
   When was you last admission?
(2) Do you suffer from any chronic medical problems?
   If yes, ...
   What treatment are you receiving? . . . .
(3) Are you on any medication at present?
   If yes, ...   dosage . . . .
   . . . .
   . . . .
(4) How many days have you experienced medical problems in the last 30? . . . .
   How many days did you not work as a result . . . .

Therapists severity rating of medical problems

No problems   Immediate hospitalisation
1   2   3   4   5   6   7   8   9   10

Employment/support status

(1) How many years of education have you completed?
(2) Have you a trade or a profession? . . . .
(3) Are you currently employed? . . . .
    If yes . . . .
    How long have you had this job? . . . .
    If less than 12 months, how many jobs have you had during the past 12
    months . . . .
    If no, are you receiving unemployment benefit? . . . .
    How long have you been receiving benefits?
(4) If employed are you experiencing problems at work?
    If yes, please specify . . . .
    How bothered are you about these problems?
    Not worried   quite worried   very worried (please tick)
(5) At present how important do you think counselling is for these problems?
    Not important   quite important   very important (please tick)
(6) How many days of work do you feel you have lost in the past 30 days
    because of your addiciton?

Therapists rating for the need for employment counselling

No Need   Urgent need
1   2   3   4   5   6   7   8   9   10

Alcohol/drug use

(1) Which of the following substances have you indulged in during the past 30
    days?

    Alcohol. . . . Heroin. . . . Other opiates. . . . Barbiturates. . . .
    Tranquilliser/sedative. . . . Cocaine. . . . Amphetamines. . . .
    Cannabis. . . . 1
    Hallucinogens. . . . Inhalants. . . . Other (please specify) . . . .

(2) Quantity and frequency of use. Daily, etc. . . . .
(3) The use of which of the above substance(s) do you consider to be a major
    problem? . . . .
(4) How long was your last period of voluntary abstinence from this substance?
    When? . . . .
(5) How many times have you:
    (a) Had alcohol DT's? . . . .
    (b) Overdosed on drugs?
(6) How many times have you been treated for:
    (a) Alcohol Abuse? . . . .   Detox . . . .
    (b) Drug Abuse? . . . .   Detox . . . .
(7) How many days have you been treated in an outpatient setting for the above
    problems? . . . .
(8) How much money would you have spent over the last 30 days on these
    substances? . . . .

Therapist rating

No problem   Severe problem
1   2   3   4   5   6   7   8   9   10

Other addictive behaviours

(1)

(2)

(3)

Therapist rating

No problems   Severe problems
1   2   3   4   5   6   7   8   9   10

Legal problems

(1) Do you have legal problems at present or have had in the past? . . . .
(2) If yes, which of the following offenses have you been charged with?
    Being drunk and disorderly. . . . Vandalism. . . . Shoplifting. . . .
    Drink/driving. . . . Drug offences. . . . . Burglary. . . . Robbery. . . . Assault. . . .
    Arson. . . . Rape. . . . Homicide/manslaughter. . . . Other (please specify) . . .
(3) How many of these charges have resulted in convictions? . . . .
    How many days, months, years have you spent in prison/remand? . . . .
(4) Are you presently awaiting trial or under probation? . . . .
    If yes, details . . . .
(5) During the past 30 days how many times have you been in trouble with the
    law? . . . .
(6) How important do you think counselling is for your legal
    problems? . . . .

Therapist rating

No problem   Severe problems
1   2   3   4   5   6   7   8   9   10

Family/social relationships

(1) Are you in a stable relationship?
    If yes, how long have you been in this relationship? . . . .
    Are you satisfied with this relationship? yes/no/don't know
(2) Which of the following is your living arrangement?
    (1) With sexual partner   (2) With sexual partner and children
    (3) With parents   (4) With family   (5) With friends   (6) Alone
    (7) Hostel   (8) No fixed abode   (9) Other . . . .
(3) How long have you had the above arrangement? . . . .
(4) With whom do you spend most of your spare time?
    (1) Family   (2) Friends   (3) Alone   (4) Other . . . .
(5) How many close friends do you have? . . . .

(6) How many days in the past 30 have you had serious conflicts?
    (a) With family ....
    (b) With other people ....
(7) How troubled or bothered have you been with?
    (a) Family problems
        Not bothered   moderately   very
    (b) Social problems
        Not bothered   moderately   very
(8) How helpful would therapy be for these problems?
    Not important   fairly important   very important

Therapist rating

No problems   Severe problems
1   2   3   4   5   6   7   8   9   10

Psychological status

(1) How many times in the past have you been treated for any psychological or emotional problems?
    (a) As an in-patient ....
    (b) As an out-patient ....
(2) Have you had a significant period (that was not a direct result of your addictive behaviour) in which you have:
    (1) Experienced serious depression   (2) Experienced serious anxiety or tension   (3) Experienced hallucinations   (4) Experienced trouble understanding, concentrating or remembering   (5) Experienced trouble controlling violent behaviour   (6) Experienced serious thoughts of suicide   (7) Attempted suicide   (8) Taken prescribed medication for any psychological or emotional problem.
(3) How many days in the past 30 have you experienced these psychological or emotional problems? ....
(4) How important is therapy for these problems?
    Not important   fairly important   very important

Therapist rating

No problems   Severe problems
1   2   3   4   5   6   7   8   9   10

Appendix A

(VI)

Example of a form that can be given to clients to list their problems at the beginning and end of treatment.

Example of a problem listing form

Please describe in your own words what you consider your most pressing
problems at present.
Please rate the severity of each problem on the 0 to 10 scale provided.

Problem 1

Severity rating
Not severe   1   2   3   4   5   6   7   8   9   10   Very severe

Problem 2

Severity rating
Not severe   1   2   3   4   5   6   7   8   9   10   Very severe

Problem 3

Severity rating
Not severe   1   2   3   4   5   6   7   8   9   10   Very severe

Problem 4

Severity rating
Not severe   1   2   3   4   5   6   7   8   9   10   Very severe

Appendix B

Useful Information

Recommended reading

Ken Back and Kate Back, (1982) *Assertiveness at Work*. McGraw Hill.

Sue Breton, (1986) *Don't Panic*. Martin Dunitz, London.

Ivy Blackburn, (1987) *Coping with Depression*. Chambers, Edinburgh.

Anthony Clare and Sally Thompson, (1981) *Let's talk about me: A critical examination of new psychotherapies*. BBC.

Valerie Curran and Susan Golombok, (1985) *Bottling It Up*. Faber & Faber.

Anne Dickson, (1982) *A woman in her own right*. Quartet.

David Fontana, (1989) *Managing Stress*. BPS, Leicester.

Ian Gawler, (1987) *Peace of Mind*. Hill of Content, Melbourne.

Lindsey Knight, (1986) *Talking to a stranger: A consumer's guide to therapy*. Fontana.

Joel Kovel, (1976) *A complete guide to therapy: From psychoanalysis to behaviour modification*. Penguin.

Peter Lambley, (1982) *Insomnia and Other Sleeping Problems*. Sphere Books, London.

Steven Levine, (1988) *A Gradual Awakening*. Century, New York.

Philip McLoone, (1988) *A Behavioural Approach to Alcohol Abuse: Practice Guidelines for Probation Officers*, Staffordshire Probation Service, South Walls, Stafford ST16 3BL.

Jane Madders, (1979) *Stress and Relaxation*. Martin Dunitz, London.

Ian Oswald and Kirstine Adam, (1983) *Get a Better Night's Sleep*. Martin Dunitz.

Dorothy Rowe, (1983) *Depression: the Way Out of Your Prison*. Routledge, London and New York.

Dorothy Rowe, (1987) *Beyond Fear*. Fontana, London.

Shirley Trickett, (1984) *Coming Off tranquillisers*. SAT Publishing, Newcastle.

A smoker's guide to giving up! Health Education Authority 78 New Oxford Street London WC1A 1AH.

Useful organisations

Alcohol Concern: 305 Grays Inn Road, London WC1X 8QF. Tel: (081) 883 3471.

British Association of Psychotherapists: 121 Hendon Lane, London N3 3PR. Tel: (081) 346 1747.

DAWN (Drugs, alcohol and women nationally): Omnibus Workspace, 39 North Road, London N7 9DP. Tel: (071) 700 4653.

DRINKWATCHERS: c/o ACCEPT, 200 Seagrave Road, London SW6 1RQ. Tel: (071) 381 3155.

Health Education Authority: 78 New Oxford Street, London WC1A 1AH.

The Institute of Alcohol Studies: Alliance House, 12 Caxton Street, London SW1H 0QS. Tel: (071) 222 4001.

ISSD (Institute for the Study of Drug Dependence): 1–4 Hatton Place, Hatton Garden, London EC1N 8ND. Tel: (071) 430 1991.

MIND: The National Association for Mental Health, 22 Harley Street, London W1N 2ED. Tel: (071) 637 0741.

National Marriage Guidance Council (Relate): Herbert Cray College, Little Church Street, Rugby, Warwicks, CV21 3AD. Tel: (0788) 73241

SCODA (Standing Conference on Drug Abuse): 1–4 Hatton Place, Hatton Garden, London EC1N 8ND. Tel: (071) 430 2341.

TACADE (Teacher's Advisory Council on Alcohol and Drug Education): Furness House, Trafford Road, Salford M5 2JX. Tel: (061) 848 0351.

Terrence Higgins Trust: 52–54 Gray's Inn Road, London WC1X 8JU. Tel: (071) 831 0330.

Women's Therapy Centre: 6 Manor Gardens, London N7 6LA. Tel: (071) 263 6200.

Self-help groups

Al-Anon and Al-Ateen: 61 Great Dover Street, London SE1 4YF. Tel: (071) 403 0888.

Alcoholics Anonymous: PO Box 514, 11 Redcliffe Gardens, London SW10 9BQ. Tel: (071) 352 3001.

ASH (Action on Smoking and Health): 5–11 Mortimer Street, London W1N 7RH. Tel: (071) 637 9843.

Co-dependents Anonymous: 67 Saverralls Road, London NW3 2LA. Tel: (071) 267 8044.

Debtors Anonymous: Tel (071) 328 4802.

Depressives Anonymous: 36 Chestnut Avenue, Beverley, North Humberside HU17 9QU. Tel: (0482) 860619.

Emotions Anonymous: Tel: (071) 722 6307 or (081) 969 2807.

Families Anonymous: 88 Caledonian Road, London N1 9DN. Tel: (081) 871 0505.

Gamblers Anonymous and Gamma Anonymous (Families and friends of gamblers): 17/23 Blantyre Street, Chenys Walk, London SW10. Tel: (071) 352 3060.

Narcotics Anonymous: PO Box 704, London SW10 0RP. Tel: (071) 351 6794.

Overeaters Anonymous: 6–9 Manor Gardens, London N7 6LA. Tel: (081) 868 4109.

Tranx, National Tranquilliser Advice Centre, 17 Peel Road, Wealdstone, Harrow, Middlesex HA3. Tel: (081) 427 2065.

Glossary

Adaptation: Adjusting to a new or variable environment. Once the environment or stimulus is repeated and ceases to be novel a response temporarily lessens, this is called *habitation*.

Addiction: A behavioural process which has physiological, cognitive and social components. This could be either a dependence on a substance or an activity. Physiological addiction/dependence is characterised by increased substance tolerance and withdrawal effects. Psychological addiction is characterised by a subjective sense of need and craving. See chapter 1.

Assertion training: Training and/or therapy, usually based on behaviour therapy, which aims to enable a person to act in his own interests, stand up for him/herself without due anxiety, and to express his rights without denying the rights of others. (From Alberti. R.E. and Emmons, M.L. (1974) *Your Perfect Right: A Guide to Assertive Behaviour.* Impact, San Luis Obispo, California.

Attribution: The explanation a person has for his or other persons behaviour.

Automatic thoughts: First described by Beck *et al.* (1979). Thoughts that occur automatically, usually in response to an event. Typically these thoughts are not questioned and at times are on the borders of awareness.

Behaviour therapy: A branch of psychotherapy narrowly conceived of as the application of classical and operant conditioning to the amelioration of clinical problems. It is more broadly conceived as applied experimental psychology.

Cognitive dissonance: Concept evolved by Festinger (1964). It refers to a state of internal tension which arises when one's beliefs, knowledge or behaviours disagree with each other. When cognitive dissonance arises, the subject is motivated to reduce it by either changing behaviour or cognitions.

Cognitive therapy: Therapy aimed at examining and changing cognitions and their underlying assumptions. It is an active, structured and directive therapy.

Compulsion: An action that a person feels driven to make and she is unable to resist.

Conditional craving: A craving response that has become associated with objects or people temporarily or actually linked to the object of craving, e.g. the spoon used to cook up heroin.

Controlled drinking: Controlled drinking is a therapeutic goal for people with a drink problem. Traditionally, abstinence was seen as the only potential therapeutic goal, however recent studies have thrown this into question. Typically, a controlled drinking programme involves an upper limit to consumption per week, and an evolution of negotiated drinking rules.

Coping: Coping refers to the process by which an individual deals with stressors. Stressors may include life events, personal problems or emotional states.

Cue exposure: A behavioral technique where objects associated with a behaviour are presented to the client. This is repeated until the exposure fails to induce a physiological or emotional response, e.g. presenting ashtray and matches to someone giving up smoking.

Denial: A cognitive manipulation used to minimise the negative consequences of ones behaviour.

Desensitisation: A behavioural technique where the client gradually imagines and is then exposed to a fear stimulus whilst deeply re-laxed. The stimuli are presented in a hierarchy from least to most feared. Sometimes referred to as systematic desensitisation.

Detoxification: A medical procedure used to gradually reduce the level of a physiologically addicted substance in the body. This is usually done by prescribing reducing amounts of the addicted substance (e.g. nicotine or heroin) or a substitute drug e.g. Methadone or Chlordiazepoxide.

Double blind: A method for eliminating the biasing effects of outcome expectations of both the subjects and experimenter. This is done by not allowing either to know whether the independent variable (the thing being tested) of the experiment is being applied to the particular subject.

Expectations: An anticipation or prediction of future events based on past experience and present stimuli. Expectations may also be biased by cognitive sets or schemas.

Humanistic: Description insight oriented psychotherapies which emphasise subjective experience and free will. Rojerian client-centred therapy is the best known of the humanistic school of therapies, this emphasises active listening, warmth and accurate empathy as the essential and active therapeutic components.

Motivational interviewing: See Chapter 7.

Personal construct theory: A theory and therapy devised by Kelly (1955). It proposes that we construct an internal model of the world, which, is then used to predict future situations.

Placebo: Any therapy, or component of a therapy which affects a person's behaviour, due to the expectation of change rather than the therapy *per se.*

Random allocation: A method of allocating subjects to groups in an experiment, that gives each subject an equal chance of being in each group. This helps ensure they are comparable before the experimental manipulation begins.

Rational emotive therapy: A cognitive therapy introduced by Albert Ellis (1955). The therapy is based on restructuring beliefs which are unrealistic. (Ellis, A. (1955) 'New approaches to psychotherapy techniques'. *Journal of Clinical Psychology*, Brandon, Vermont.)

Rationalisation: A cognitive manipulation used to defend oneself from the strength of emotional feelings.

Self-efficacy: The belief that a person can respond effectively to a situation by using available skills.

Self-esteem: A self-evaluation, which is often conceptualised as the psychological distance between one's ideal self and actual self.

Self-monitoring: A technique whereby the client records specific behaviours or thoughts on a (usually) tailor-made record form. This usually also covers antecedents and on sequences of the behaviour or thoughts.

State dependent learning: Chapter 11.

Stress: A stimulus which strains the physiological or psychological capacities of an organism.

Stress inoculation training: Training which gradually exposes subjects to stressors to increase the range and strength of their coping techniques.

Thinking errors: Where particular patterns of thinking are dysfunctional for an individual.

Vigilance: The capacity to attend, without minimal distraction to a task.

Index